ISBN 1-877331-77-5

ORGANISE WORKPLACE INFORMATION

Software Publications

Organise workplace information

© Copyright Software Educational Resources Ltd, January 2003

Author: Cheryl Price

T.Dip.WP, T.Dip.T

Julia Wix

T.Dip.WP

Jan Haine

MOS Instructor, T.Dip.ITS, Cert SMgt

ISBN: 1-877331-77-5

Disclaimer

Publishers – Software Publications Pty Ltd (ABN 75 078 026 150)

Head Office – Sydney
Unit 10, 171 Gibbes Street
Chatswood NSW 2067
Australia

Web Address
www.softwarepublications.com

Branches

Adelaide, Brisbane, Melbourne, Perth and Auckland

Downloading Exercise Files

Exercise files that are used with this book are available for free download from our web site.

1   Click on the Start button, select Programs then click on Internet Explorer
     OR double click on Internet Explorer (OR Netscape Navigator) on your Desktop.

2   If the Dial-up Connection dialog box appears, type in your Username and Password and click on Connect.

3   When you are connected, click in the Address box of your browser and type:

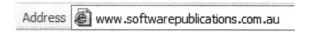

4   Press Enter.

     The Software Publications web site will be displayed on screen.

5   Click on **Exercise Files**.

6   Click on **Instructions**. Click on **Downloading Instructions**.

7   Click on Open.

8   Click on the **Print** button so you can use these instructions to install the exercise files onto your computer.

9   Click on the **Back** button twice to return to the exercise files web page.

10   Click on the required category.

11   Select the relevant exercise file/s. (Exercise files are compressed into one file.)

12   Use the printed instructions to install the exercise files onto your computer.

     Instructions are given to install the files into My Documents folder. If you are on a network these files may need to be copied to another location.

Introduction

This book may be used as a stand-alone text, or in conjunction with our book *Produce Business Documents – BSBCMN306A.*

The student will learn how to manage information in an organisation using a range of tools, including Word, Excel, PowerPoint and Outlook 2002 from the MS Office XP suite.

In addition, file management issues are addressed using Windows Explorer in Windows XP. An existing basic skill level in Word and Excel is assumed; in the case of all other applications, step-by-step instructions ensure that even a new user will be able to successfully complete the exercises.

A practical, real-world approach is facilitated through the use of a fictitious organisation (Care Cosmetics), where one main information management issue is identified and addressed throughout the book. Additional exercises not relating to Care Cosmetics provide skill consolidation opportunities.

Scenario

Care Cosmetics sells a variety of skin care, skin repair, hair care and herbal therapy products. The organisation sells its product to wholesalers using travelling sales representatives, and also directly to the public through its own retail branches where a range of professional consultation services are also offered.

The rapid growth of the organisation has resulted in three new branches being opened in the past year, the integration of the existing Sydney branches into satellite centres of one Sydney branch, and the likelihood of several more branches being opened over the next 12 months.

Care Cosmetics has a wide range of existing information relating to its operation, held in many different formats. The informal way in which information has been collected and used in the past is no longer sufficient to meet the needs of the growing organisation.

One of the main problems is the lack of reliable sales information provided by branches to Head Office. Branch managers collect and use their own information independently without any formal reporting to a central point.

At the Melbourne branch, the manager provides his staff with a form that they are required to keep up to date during the day, recording details of the number of sales made. The manager or one of his staff totals the daily results at the end of each week, resulting in a total sales result per staff member each week.

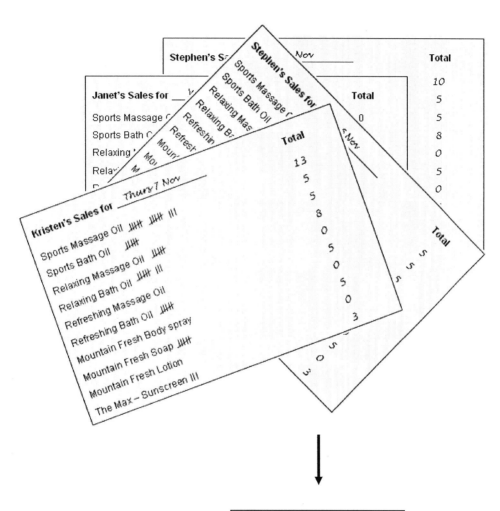

The Sydney branch manager has overall responsibility for the main branch in the heart of Sydney, as well as the four satellite centres located in outlying areas. The entire Sydney operation, as well as Head Office which is also located there, uses the company's original accounting system. The newer branches in Brisbane, Melbourne and Perth use a different accounting package, and the two systems are not linked at this stage. Over the next year, it is planned to bring the Sydney operation and Head Office into the new accounting system, effectively replacing the old one.

The Sydney branch manager downloads a trial balance once a month, where she can immediately see the dollar value of sales during the month. She always sends an email to Head Office advising them of this figure.

```
Trial Balance for
Care Cosmetics - Sydney Branches
30 September 2002

                  YTD Debit      YTD Credit

Sales
   Skin care                        13,560
   Cosmetics                         7,664
   Other                              861
                      22,085
```

→

✉ Sales results for September - Message (Plain Text)
File Edit View Insert Format Tools Actions Help
Send

To...   LindaH@CareCosmetics.com.au
Cc...
Bcc...
Subject: Sales results for September

Hi Linda,

Sales for the month were $22,085

Regards,
Sarah Linehan
Sydney Branch Manager

At the Brisbane branch, a sales meeting is held every morning, at which targets are set for the day. Every staff member's targets are loaded into a spreadsheet, which also has room for the number and dollar value of sales to be recorded during the day. The spreadsheet automatically calculates the percentage of target achieved, so that staff can track their progress at any time. Every spreadsheet is printed at the end of every day, and this forms the basis for the next day's sales meeting and targets. The manager compiles weekly spreadsheets from the daily results, and a monthly summary from the weekly results. The spreadsheet containing weekly results is posted on a notice board in the reception area so that staff and clients can clearly see what has been achieved by the branch. Whenever Head Office asks for sales information, the manager is able to instantly provide whatever is required in a very presentable spreadsheet, as he is a skilled user of Excel.

The Perth branch manager collects a range of information about sales results from daily informal interviews with her staff. Once a week, she takes her notes home, and her son enters the figures into a spreadsheet that he has created for the purpose on their home computer.

The Head Office management team needs to be able to track the dollar value of actual sales from all branches every month. They need to compare branch results, and compare results from one month to the next. The collated sales information will be presented at monthly management meetings, and needs to be held in a format which will enable easy sharing with branch managers and staff.

Table of Contents

Section Two – Organise Information

Section Five – Review Information Needs

Section

1

Collect and Assess Information

Learning Outcomes

At the end of this section you should be able to -

❑   Use reliable and efficient methods of collecting information.

❑   Collect information from teams and individuals using participative techniques and appropriate interpersonal skills.

❑   Assess information held by an organisation for relevance to the organisation's requirements.

❑   Ensure that information collected is suitable for analysis, decision making and the development of plans, strategies and options.

Introduction

Information is one of the cornerstones of any organisation, so learning to manage it effectively is a key business skill.

In this section, you will learn:

- What and how information arrives in an organisation
- What information is needed to solve a problem
- How to collect information
- How to ensure information collected is appropriate to the requirements of an organisation and is suitable for its final purpose.

Information Procedures in Organisations

Although there are many different types of organisations, most have similar procedures in the way that incoming and outgoing information is managed.

Incoming Information

There are many different avenues through which information can arrive in an organisation.

They include:

- The postal service
- Courier delivery
- Verbal (telephone, face to face)
- Electronic mail (email)
- The Internet
- Facsimile machine (fax)

General Offices

In a general office information is usually received by all the above methods. The type of information will vary depending on the type of organisation and their activities.

Schools

A school office will receive information from various sources: from within the school itself, from the Department of Education, parents and salespeople. Information is usually received by a combination of the above methods.

Retail Outlets

Shops will receive accounts, bank statements, requests from customers, and product information from suppliers. These documents will arrive through a variety of communication systems (telephone, mail, courier, customer).

Remote Offices

Sales representatives are an example of people who may complete most of their work from a vehicle, rather than from a traditional office. They receive product information from businesses they represent. In addition, they will obtain orders from customers and requests for visits through the main business office. In a remote office, information may be sent and received via phone, fax, laptop computer or PDA. (See Section 2 to find out more about the business equipment and technologies used to deal with information in an organisation.)

Home Based Offices

Self-employed or other home-based workers will receive instructions from clients or their employer regarding the type of work they are undertaking. Items such as bills, advertising material, products, etc, will arrive through a variety of communication media, frequently involving courier, telephone, fax, and often a heavy reliance on email and computers.

In all cases, an office provides a location for information to be received at or sent from.

Information Overload

Too much incoming information is a growing problem in organisations. Computers have made it possible to collect and distribute vast amounts of information with ease, and in many organisations this is exactly what occurs – information is collected and distributed indiscriminately, with little regard for the relevance and usefulness of it.

It is essential to keep a clear focus on why information is being held – what purpose does it serve, and does it do the job for which it was intended?

Actively managing the information in an organisation ensures that the quality remains high and that only useful information is retained.

Exercise 1

Provide three examples of irrelevant information that may arrive in an organisation, each by a different avenue (see *Incoming Information* on page 2).

1 ....

2 ....

3 ....

What Information is Needed?

Before collecting any information, it is essential to establish:

- what information is required
- what is the best way to collect the information
- what tool(s) will be the most appropriate to organise and manipulate the information.

Exercise 2

Read the scenario at the beginning of the book. The overall problem presented (ie the lack of credible sales information) lends itself to being resolved, at least in part, by a spreadsheet in which sales information can be collected, organised, manipulated and re-distributed in a useful format.

Spreadsheet Development

The process of developing a spreadsheet to solve an information-related problem is shown at the right.

A problem has been identified as solvable by a spreadsheet. A brief is created; a working plan is then made from the brief. Using the working plan, a spreadsheet is created. Documentation relating to the spreadsheet is written. The outcomes of the spreadsheet are presented for evaluation.

Problem

First you need to determine the problem, then you can decide whether it is solvable by a spreadsheet.

Brief

If the problem is identified as solvable by a spreadsheet, a brief is created.

A brief includes:

- Desirable outcomes
- Identification of constraints
- Particular specifications relating to the spreadsheet
- Information on whether charts and macros are to be included
- Any organisational requirements (style, location of file, etc)
- Purpose of the spreadsheet
- The target user(s) of the spreadsheet

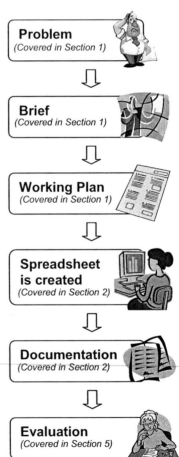

Problem
(Covered in Section 1)

Brief
(Covered in Section 1)

Working Plan
(Covered in Section 1)

Spreadsheet is created
(Covered in Section 2)

Documentation
(Covered in Section 2)

Evaluation
(Covered in Section 5)

Working Plan

A working plan is created from the brief and usually includes the purpose of the spreadsheet, spreadsheet features to be used, a sketch of the spreadsheet with the specifications and the location of the file (including file name).

Create the Spreadsheet

(covered in Section 2)

The spreadsheet can be created from the working plan in a spreadsheet program such as Microsoft Excel. Data is entered, and formulas and charts created. All formulas and data should be double checked for accuracy.

Documentation

(covered in Section 2)

Information about the spreadsheet should be documented either in the worksheet, on a separate worksheet or in a word processing document. The documentation is then available to assist users of the spreadsheet.

Evaluation

(covered in Section 5)

Evaluation is used to determine whether the spreadsheet has solved the problem. This includes deciding whether the:

- spreadsheet complies with the brief
- spreadsheet is appropriately formatted and presented
- data in the spreadsheet is readable and legible
- spreadsheet calculations and data are accurate
- appropriate data integrity practices have been implemented

On the next few pages you will work through an example of a problem, brief and working plan. In Section 2 you will create a spreadsheet and complete documentation for it. Finally, you will evaluate your work in Section 5.

An Example of Spreadsheet Development

This example shows the first steps of the development of a spreadsheet. Read and understand the example before you begin to create your own spreadsheet solution for Care Cosmetics' sales results.

Problem

Three staff members at Care Cosmetics require mobile phones.

Each staff member has a total budget for a phone. This amount must cover the initial purchase of the phone handset and the first month's account payment. In addition, it must cover any extra costs of accessories that the staff member needs. Each staff member has done some research and found two phone packages that fit their needs. The finance staff need to plan a spreadsheet that will tell them whether the two packages come in under budget.

Claire Simpson   Claire is an account manager for Care Cosmetics. Claire's budget is $950. Claire has found the following packages. A Nokia 5510 phone costs $599. The monthly charge is $120 and the extras that she requires (a hands free car kit and phone cover) cost $160. Claire's second suggestion is a Siemens ME45. This model costs $869, but the monthly cost is only $100. The extras are on special offer for this model and cost only $100.

Richard Fuller   A delivery truck driver, Richard needs a phone to take with him when he distributes products to Care Cosmetics' clients. A budget of $520 has been allocated for Richard's phone. Richard has identified the first model that he would be happy with as the Alcatel 511. The handset costs $379 and the monthly charge is $80. He needs a hands free car kit and this costs $50. Richard's second choice is the Nokia 3315. This retails at $349, but the monthly charge is $120. The car kit costs $70.

Brent Hampton   Brent is a student working at Care Cosmetics. The company has agreed to purchase a phone for him in return for his promise to return to work for them in the Christmas holiday. Brent has a total budget of $230. His first choice is the Alcatel 311, retailing at $219. The monthly charge is $15 as he only requires off-peak calling. Brent's second choice is the Ericsson A3618. The handset for this costs $199 and the monthly charge is $20. Brent does not require any extras or accessories.

The problem to be solved is: *Which mobile phone package can be bought with the budget set for each employee?*

Create a Brief

Exercise 3

    Use the bullet points on page 4 to create a brief for the mobile phones scenario.

....

....

....

....

....

....

....

....

....

Working Plan

Exercise 4

On the next page is an example of a working plan created from a brief.

Read the working plan and understand how it relates to the problem and to your brief.

Spreadsheet Working Plan

Purpose

The purpose of the spreadsheet is to identify an appropriately priced mobile phone package for each of the following staff members – Claire Simpson, Richard Fuller and Brent Hampton.

Spreadsheet features to be used

AutoSum, Chart, Borders, fonts, Macros (to print worksheet data and another to print just the chart)

Spreadsheet Specifications

Mobile Phone Packages									
		Mobile Phone	Phone	Monthly	Extra	Initial			
		Model	Cost	Cost	Costs	Cost			
Claire	Package 1			→		=sum( )			
	Package 2			→		=sum( )			
Richard	Package 1			→		=sum( )			
	Package 2			→		=sum( )			
Brent	Package 1			→		=sum( )			
	Package 2			→		=sum( )			
Chart Initial Costs – separate worksheet									

File name and Location of Spreadsheet

C:\My Documents\equipment purchases\Mobile Phone Packages

Exercise 5

 Use the Care Cosmetics scenario at the beginning of the book (see *Introduction*) to complete the first three steps of developing a spreadsheet solution.

1 Identify the problem to be solved. Write it below in your own words.

....

....

....

....

2 Create a handwritten brief.

3 Create a working plan using the form on the next page.

Spreadsheet Working Plan

Purpose

....

....

....

Spreadsheet features to be used

....

....

....

Spreadsheet Specifications

File name and Location of Spreadsheet

....

....

....

Personal Collection of Information

When the type of information required has been established, the next consideration is *how* the information will be collected, for example, in person or in writing. The key to the quality of any information collected *in person* is how well relevant interpersonal skills are used in the process. These skills apply in a wide range of situations, including one-to-one conversations in person or over the telephone, team meetings, and interviews with clients or suppliers.

Communication and interpersonal skills include:

- Body language
- Listening
- Verbal communication
- Questioning techniques

Body Language

What is Body Language?

We are all trained in the use of speech to communicate what we mean in a way that other people will understand. Most of the time, others understand what we mean. In a telephone conversation, we communicate through speech alone but in a face-to-face meeting, part of the communication is carried on in a non-verbal form, often called *body language*.

The key aspects of body language are:

- Eye contact
- Posture
- Body position
- Personal space
- Actions and gestures
- Facial expressions

The Importance of Body Language

There are two principal reasons why body language is important.

1   People *remember* more of what they see than what they hear.

2   People tend to *believe* what they see rather than what they hear because body language is seen as being more honest. When words and body language say different things, we tend to believe the body language and doubt the words.

Communicating with Body Language

Take the position of your body as an example.

- You can face towards the speaker, making eye contact. Alternatively, you may face to the side but have one foot forward pointing towards the speaker. These signs indicate that you are interested in what the speaker has to say and want to hear more.

- You can lean backwards or turn to the side with no feet facing the speaker. This has very negative implications and shows a lack of interest – or boredom. If you have your arms crossed or are looking down towards the ground, this creates even more of a barrier between you and the speaker.

- You can turn away from the speaker during the conversation or – worst of all – turn your back on the speaker and address him/her over your shoulder. This is very negative and shows that you have lost interest in the conversation and want to get away.

Project a Positive Image

Body language is essential in communicating a positive image. For example, look at the people in the table below - how would you interpret their body language? Do you agree with our comments?

	We suggest:
 Confident and friendly	These two friends are facing towards each other and are making friendly eye contact. They are looking at each other but probably breaking eye contact every few seconds so as not to be too intense. This is the ideal way to address other people. It is friendly and interested but not threatening or aggressive.
 Aggressive and unpleasantly intense	This staring pair of eyes is guaranteed to make the other person uncomfortable!

Exercise 6

Based on your knowledge so far, list two key aspects of body language and briefly explain the meaning of each.

1 ....

....

....

....

2 ....

....

....

....

Take a look at the following table to see how aspects of our body language can be either positive or negative.

Eye contact		
Positive		**Negative**
Making frequent eye contact indicates interest.		Staring will make people uncomfortable and can seem threatening.
		Avoiding eye contact will make you appear shifty and/or bored and disinterested.
Posture		
Positive		**Negative**
A relaxed posture indicates no major barriers to communication.		A tense body can indicate concern with the topic or in dealing with the other person.
Body position		
Positive		**Negative**
Facing forward, with shoulders and feet facing the other party, or body facing to one side, but with one foot pointing towards the other person, shows interest and a desire to listen.		Body and both feet facing to the side indicate disinterest and desire to get away. Turning one's back shows great keenness to be elsewhere.
Personal space		
Positive		**Negative**
Leaning closer to reduce the distance between two people indicates growing interest.		Leaning away can indicate a lack of interest or agreement with what is being said. Encroaching on personal space is threatening.

Actions		
Positive		**Negative**
Uncrossed arms and hands open (palms up or otherwise visible to the other person) are signs of openness.		Arms folded in front of one's body creates a barrier and can express resistance to what is being said.
Nodding signals agreement, interest and understanding.		Fidgeting, yawning or being distracted is usually a sign of boredom, nervousness or impatience. The other person is talking too much or in too much technical detail.
Taking notes shows interest and involvement.		Biting nails or nervous tapping with the fingers indicates nervousness and worry or concern at what is being said.
Smiling/adding humour signals a warm personal relationship.		A hand over one's mouth or leaning on one's elbow with the chin in the hand can communicate boredom.
Using the hands to gesture indicates involvement in the conversation and openness to the other person.		Trying to interrupt what the other person is saying or opening one's mouth frequently as if to speak, shows impatience.

Facial expressions		
Positive		**Negative**
Smiling shows warmth and interest and encourages the speaker to continue with what they are saying.		Wrinkled brow and frowning indicates non-agreement with what is being said or discomfort with the speaker's opinions.

Exercise 7

1   Write the following words on individual pieces of paper and give them to four different people.

- Polite and professional
- Shifty and suspicious looking
- Shy
- Angry

2   Let the class know what each piece of paper says, but not who has which piece of paper.

3   Identify something in the room, and ask each of the four people to describe it. They can use the same, or similar, words but must use body language appropriate to the character described on their piece of paper.

4   Ask the class to guess which person has which character.

1   Which of three girls below looks as though she is listening to you properly?

....

Harriet   **Jane**   **Emma**

2   Explain the reasons for your answer above, commenting on the body language of each girl.

....

....

....

....

Effective Listening Skills

It is often said that the best communicators are those who spend more time *listening* than speaking. People like to talk and like to feel that they are being taken seriously. If you listen to people, they feel that you respect them and are interested in what they have to say. They will be happier to share ideas and information with you and are more likely to be co-operative.

By listening effectively, you gain more information and knowledge.

There are four stages to the listening process.

1   **Hear** At this stage, you simply pay attention to make sure you have heard the message. Do not interrupt the speaker or put limitations on your listening time, or the speaker will get the impression that you are not interested in what they are saying.

2   **Interpret** Decide what the speaker means. Failure to interpret the speaker's words correctly, frequently leads to misunderstanding. People sometimes interpret words differently because of varying experience, knowledge, vocabulary, culture, background, and attitude. A good speaker uses tone of voice, facial expressions, and mannerisms to help make the message clear to the listener.

3   **Evaluate** Decide what to do with the information you have received. For example, when listening to a sales pitch, you have two options: you can choose either to believe or to disbelieve the salesperson.

4   **Respond**   This is a verbal or visual response to indicate that you have understood the message and your reaction to it.

Become a Better Listener

To communicate better, concentrate on listening more effectively. The following pointers will help.

Confirm your understanding   Imagine you are a tape recorder. Try to play back the speaker's words accurately. Restating the speaker's concepts will help you to concentrate and you will indicate to the speaker that you understand correctly.

"As I understand it, the problem is …" *or* "Do you mean...?"

You are reassuring the speaker that you are both talking about the same thing.

Clarify by asking questions   If there is something you do not understand, ASK.

Do not jump to conclusions   Many people tune a speaker out when they think they have the gist of the conversation or know what he or she is going to say next. However, the speaker may not be following the same train of thought as you, or not planning to make the point you assume. If you do not listen, you may miss the real message.

Read the speaker's body language   People do not always say what they mean, but their body language is usually an accurate indication of their intention. Many clues to meaning come from the speaker's tone of voice, their facial expressions and gestures. For example, your boss may want to advise you that you dress rather too scruffily. S/he may use light-hearted words (so as not to appear too heavy-handed), but the body language might indicate that you should not be misled into thinking that the message is not serious.

Be aware of your own body language   Make eye contact – it helps you to focus on the message, not the environment, and will draw the speaker out to give information.

Do not let yourself be distracted   Do not be distracted by the environment or the speaker's appearance, accent or mannerisms.

Keep an open mind   Do not only listen for statements that back up your own opinions and support your beliefs, or for certain parts that interest you. The point of listening, after all, is to gain new information.

Provide feedback   Encouraging, non-committal statements will keep a speaker comfortable. The speaker will appreciate your interest and feel that you are really listening.

"I see" *or* "Mmm, carry on."

Go in with a positive attitude   To get the most out of a meeting, speech, or conversation, say to yourself, "What can I learn from this to make me more valuable in my industry and to my organisation?"

Exercise 9

1   Imagine you work in a DIY shop and a customer said to you "I like your range of paints for house interiors, but of course wallpaper is what everyone seems to be using these days". Make brief notes about the four stages of the listening process after hearing this comment.

1   Hearing   ....

2   Interpretation ....

3   Evaluation   ....

4   Response   ....

2   What extra information would you like to find out from the customer before taking any action?

....

....

....

....

Exercise 10

Form a pair with another person and name yourselves Person 1 and Person 2.

1   Person 1 describes the plot of their favourite film to Person 2.

2   When Person 1 has finished, Person 2 describes the plot of their favourite film, and Person 1 listens.

3   When both have finished, each person writes down the plot of the film, as it was described by the other.

How effectively did you listen to the other person? What could you have done better?

....

....

....

....

....

....

Active Listening for Better Communication

Active listening is an excellent technique to use when gathering complex information.

The listener concentrates fully on what the speaker is saying, and then repeats, in the listener's own words, what he or she thinks the speaker has said.

The purpose of this is to ensure that both the speaker and listener know that the speaker has been understood. The listener does not have to agree with what is being said, but must make it clear what he or she understands is being said.

Active listening has several benefits.

- It forces you to listen attentively to the speaker. If you know you will have to repeat something in your own words, you tend to concentrate harder.

- It avoids misunderstandings, as you have to confirm that you really do understand what the speaker has said.

- It tends to encourage the speaker to say more.

Active listening uses the following techniques.

- Encouraging
- Rephrasing
- Summarising

Encourage

You might encourage the speaker by using eye contact, positive body language, and saying things like "I see…", "Uh huh", or "That's interesting". You are not agreeing or disagreeing, but are showing your interest and encouraging the other person to keep talking.

Rephrase

Rephrasing means saying the same thing as the speaker, but using different words. This is to show your understanding of the facts, or the argument. If you have misunderstood, the speaker has an opportunity to correct you.

Keyword: Rephrase

To rephrase a sentence is to repeat it, using different words. In conversation, this can help ensure that both people understand what is being said.

Example

Chris and Lyn are reviewing last week's sales results for Care Cosmetics.

By rephrasing Chris' original statement, Lyn is making sure she fully understands what Chris is saying. In this case, Lyn has slightly misunderstood, and Chris is given the opportunity to explain.

Exercise 11

Rephrase the following statements.

"That wallpaper is mind-blowing!"

....

....

"Our new range of cosmetics is going to knock your socks off".

....

....

"I see that your skin analysis consultation takes a whole hour."

....

....

"Sales of our new anti-ageing sunscreen are off the planet!"

....

....

Summarise

You summarise what the speaker has said by briefly pulling all the important facts together, when he or she has finished speaking.

You might say "These seem to be the main points you have made…", or "So to summarise, you would like me to…".

Exercise 12

The Customer Service Manager at Care Cosmetics has the following conversation with one of his staff.

"I'd like to hold a *Customer Focus Group* meeting next month. I think we should invite the four biggest spending customers, and two customers that we have recently lost. Can you check the sales records? We can fit in two more – I'd like to choose two who have sent in suggestions by email; you will know who is appropriate. I'll need to draft an agenda by the end of the week and for that I need a summary of comments from our suggestion boxes and from the website feedback form. Can you get me all the information by Wednesday lunchtime, please?"

Summarise the key information that the staff member needs to ensure the Customer Service Manager's request is met.

....

....

....

....

....

....

....

....

Ineffective Listening

When it comes to listening, many of us are guilty of at least some bad habits. For example, tick the boxes if you do any of the following:

❑ Instead of listening while someone is talking, do you think about what you are going to say next?

❑ Are you easily distracted by the speaker's mannerisms or what is going on around you?

❑ Do you frequently interrupt people before they have finished talking?

❑ Do you drift off into daydreams because you are sure you know what the speaker is going to say?

All of these habits can hinder our listening ability. Contrary to popular notion, listening is not a passive activity. It requires full concentration and active involvement and is, in fact, hard work.

Exercise 13

➢ Check your listening skills by reading through these comments (or have someone read them out loud to you, if possible), then indicate whether you think the statements which follow are true or false.

1   Customer to sales department: "I'd like to meet up with one of your account managers when they visit my area. I have a few questions about your products that I would like to ask."

	True	False
Your products probably aren't right for this customer.	❑	❑
The customer is not particularly impressed with your products.	❑	❑
The customer has already decided to buy some of your products.	❑	❑

2   Sales Manager to staff member: "Your sales results for last month were impressive – how would you feel about increasing your targets for this month to see if you can do even better?"

	True	False
The sales manager believes his staff member is not working as hard as he could be.	❑	❑
The sales manager is pleased with his staff member's results.	❑	❑
The sales manager wants to offer his staff member a challenge to do better.	❑	❑

3   New branch manager to an experienced branch manager: "I can't believe your sales results – how do you motivate your staff to perform at that level consistently?"

	True	False
The new manager doesn't believe that the sales results produced at the experienced manager's branch are correct.	❑	❑
The new manager wants to learn from the experienced branch manager.	❑	❑
The new manager is concerned that the experienced manager's staff are being pushed too hard and expectations of them are too high.	❑	❑

Verbal Communication

If you plan to collect information verbally, careful thought needs to be applied to what you say, and how you word your request. Consider the following points.

Voice

- Your voice mirrors your personality and feeling. It indicates your mood. If you are tired and grouchy, your voice reflects that.

- Have peaks and valleys in your voice for interesting contrast. This helps to hold attention. Keep the less important words in the valleys.

- Put a smile in your voice and be enthusiastic.

- Speak clearly – do not make people strain to hear you.

Words and Etiquette

- Always be courteous and polite.

- Choose the right phrases – "Is now a good time for us to talk about sales results for your branch, Brian?" will elicit a better response than "I'm phoning to get your sales results."

Exercise 14

Read the following sentence out loud, putting emphasis on the first word.

I'M sorry, we do not open on Saturdays.

Then say it again with the emphasis on the second word:

I'm **SORRY**, we do not open on Saturdays.

See how the meaning changes? It now sounds quite aggressive and perhaps a little sarcastic – as though you are not sorry at all.

It is important to get the tone of your voice right and to emphasise the right words – otherwise your words could be taken in the wrong way.

Try emphasising other words in the sentence:

> I'm sorry, **WE** do not open on Saturdays (…but our competitors do).
>
> I'm sorry, we **DO NOT** open on Saturdays (…aren't you listening?).
>
> I'm sorry, we do not **OPEN** on Saturdays (…we're shut, leave us alone).

Now you can see how important the tone of your voice is.

Exercise 15

Answer the following questions.

1   Why are verbal communication skills important for a sales representative?

   ....
   ....
   ....

2   Give two examples of positive verbal communication and two examples of negative verbal communication. What do they tell you about the other person?

Positive

a. ....

....

b. ....

....

Negative

a. ....

....

b. ....

....

Questioning Techniques

Listening is only part of making sure that we get the right information from people. In order to ensure that correct and relevant information is obtained, the right questions must be asked.

The following are the main types of question and when to ask them.

Closed Questions

Closed questions are those that produce a limited range of answers, often Yes or No, and are used to establish something definite. They tend to begin with Can, Did, Do, Have, Is, Will and Would. Closed questions are useful in order to elicit information that is uncontroversial and does not need much discussion. However, used in an inappropriate situation, closed questions can cause frustration and prevent the communication of useful information.

Open Questions

Open questions are designed to produce more detailed answers. For instance "How did last week's sales results look?" would probably produce a fuller answer than a closed question such as "Did your branch do well last week?"

Open questions are useful for generating interesting and useful discussion. This is a better type of question to ask when trying to collect information. Open questions tend to start with How, What, When, Where, Who, Why.

By using an open question, you are encouraging the other person to think about the issue and perhaps to consider solutions to problems. By doing so, you will get more out of that person. For instance, if sales results have not been collated for you to collect, do not ask "Didn't you have time to collate the results?" Instead, try "Why weren't you able to collate the results?"

Exercise 16

For each of the closed questions below, suggest an open question alternative.

Closed: "Is it possible that you didn't reach target due to staff shortages?"

Open: ....

Closed: "Do you think we should reward staff who achieve budget with an incentive scheme?"

Open: ....

Closed: "Are you happy with the sales targets for next year?"

Open: ....

Closed: "Do you think we should incorporate more of our products into the sales we are asking staff to target?"

Open: ....

Leading Questions

When collecting information, avoid questions that expect a particular answer and might therefore lead the person into answering untruthfully or unthinkingly. For example, if you were asked:

> "You achieved target this month, didn't you?"

… you might not want to admit that you actually hadn't.

Similarly, if you were asked:

> "We didn't get the sales results through from your branch yesterday as required, but you weren't in the office at all yesterday, were you?"

… you may agree without really thinking about the question, because the speaker obviously thinks you were not in the office yesterday. If you thought harder you might remember having called in to the office at lunchtime and noticing one of your staff sending the results by fax.

Double Questions

Beware of "double questions" that actually require a complex answer to more than one clear point.

> "Is it the case that our marketing campaign hasn't been very successful, or are all our competitors finding the market to be very slow?"

The listener would find this a confusing question to answer as there are two different issues rolled into one question. Whether the campaign was unsuccessful or whether competitors are finding the market to be very slow are separate matters.

Exercise 17

Suggest an open question that the following people might ask to find out what their customers want.

1   A real estate agent

    ....

    ....

2   A painter and decorator

    ....

    ....

3   A training course presenter

    ....

    ....

4   A fitness instructor

    ....

    ....

5   A wedding caterer

    ....

    ....

6   A Care Cosmetics sales representative

    ....

    ....

    ....

Direct Methods of Collecting Information

When the type of information required has been established, a system needs to be put in place to collect it. There are many possible information collection methods, including interviews and conversations, meetings, accessing information held by other organisations, and the use of formal or informal written methods.

Meetings

Meetings can be:

- with staff or clients;
- in large or small groups, or one-to-one;
- face-to-face, by telephone, or using a computer with software designed to allow remote users to "meet" online using an Internet connection.

Manage Staff Meetings

In any team it is important for the team members to get to know and understand one another. Some people will be quiet, and appear not to contribute to information-gathering or decision-making. Is this because they feel the group is dominated by one or two strong individuals? Make sure everyone has the chance to contribute – quieter personalities may find it easier to make suggestions via email, or on a one-to-one basis, and may feel intimidated in a group situation.

In any group situation certain behaviours will become apparent. One or two team members might have loud, dominant personalities – they may talk a great deal, and like to have their own way. While this may be annoying to others, it is important to realise that this is part of their personality, and they may be unable to work any other way. Another might take on the role of "class clown" – this is a behaviour they have developed over the years, and it is how they feel most comfortable.

It is vital that every member of the team is aware of what is expected of them at a team meeting, eg if they have to produce a progress report, should this be a written report (to be circulated to all members) or is a verbal report sufficient?

Understand Teamwork

If your choice of information collection method involves meeting with others, it is essential to have a firm grasp of how teams work together.

There are very few jobs where you can work in complete isolation. It is therefore essential to learn how to work with other people. In some cases you may not particularly like the people in your team, but in order for your project to be successful you have to learn to work with them. The departmental manager is usually the person who assigns members to a team, based on the required skills. If you are at first wary of other team members, you should realise that they probably think the same about you, and expect you to demonstrate why you were selected to be part of the team.

A group of people working together on a project will generate energy and produce a high level of commitment, but it is important to understand that a successful team does not just happen – it requires work, and every team member is responsible for helping to achieve the synergy that a successful team can produce. Team members may have to learn to function as a team before they actually start work on their project.

Share Information and Ideas

In a team, tasks should ideally be allocated fairly. Sometimes a team member will have specific skills and it is reasonable to expect that related tasks will be allocated to that individual. However, in other cases, such as a group assignment, there could be four tasks requiring equivalent time and effort to be allocated among four group members.

In some group situations, the entire team may work together on collecting information. A group meeting will need to be held, and brainstorming begins. A potential problem with this situation is that shy group members will not contribute, and the more dominant, talkative ones (but not necessarily the ones with the best ideas or correct information) will take over. Also, there could be one or more lazy group member(s) who decide they do not have to contribute at all, are absent from group meetings, and turn up at the end to collect the credit! The team will have to evaluate each other and put pressure on the negligent members to toe the line.

Respect the Speaking Rights of Others

In any group there will be one or two people who love the sound of their own voice, and consider that what they have to say is of far more importance than any other person's contribution.

Tactics to manage this type of issue could include:

- Setting a time limit on each topic;

- Insisting on a decision when the time limit is up, even if it is only to defer the final decision until the next meeting, or that some of the members will research the topic further and bring the results to the next meeting;

- Permitting each person three minutes only on each topic;

- Permitting everyone only one opportunity (initially) to comment on a topic;

- Instigating a rule that everyone in the group is given the chance to contribute, without interruptions or put-downs.

Exercise 18

Think about the sales information that must be collected from Care Cosmetics' branches. (You may wish to re-read the scenario at the beginning of the book.)

List three potential advantages of holding a meeting to explain the type of information required to branch managers.

1 ....

....

2 ....

....

3 ....

....

List three potential disadvantages of holding a meeting to address the issue.

1 ....

....

2 ....

....

3 ....

....

Exercise 19

Write some notes on how you would conduct the meeting discussed in Exercise 18, taking the points you have made in that exercise into account. Note who would attend the meeting, what information would be given to participants and in what form, and what requests would be made of the participants both during and subsequent to the meeting.

....

....

....

....

....

....

....

....

....

....

....

....

Effective Conversation

A good conversation can go on for hours, or last for a few seconds. Either way, the test of its effectiveness is: Did it achieve its objectives?

A conversation is the informal exchange of information or ideas using the spoken word. It might be between two people or a whole group of people.

Objectives could include:

- building a rapport
- discovering other people's opinions
- making your opinion known and persuading others to agree
- collecting or giving information
- teaching or coaching

Build a Rapport

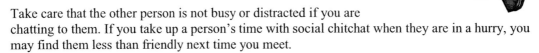

Getting to know an individual can be useful as it can improve customer and/or staff relations. However, being too friendly may be inappropriate if you have serious business to discuss in a work setting.

Take care that the other person is not busy or distracted if you are chatting to them. If you take up a person's time with social chitchat when they are in a hurry, you may find them less than friendly next time you meet.

Social conversation can centre on almost any topic. Try picking a subject you find interesting and that the other person has shown a strong interest in too. Look out for mutual interests, similar experiences, and shared attitudes. These will form good subjects for conversation.

Obviously, there are some subjects you should avoid, including confidential information, gossip and controversial topics (politics, religion etc).

Exchange Opinions and Use Persuasion

If you are keen to find out another person's opinion on something, make your own opinion known, or perhaps persuade others to agree with your viewpoint, the first and most important thing is: It is not a contest, so relax, and keep an open mind.

- The purpose of discussion with customers or those with whom you work is to come up with a solution that works best. You are not taking part in a debating competition, and you certainly should not regard the other person as an opponent. You are on the same side, and should behave as such. Be ready to change, or modify, your opinion if that is best for your organisation or for the task in hand.

- Often, it is not the argument itself that puts people off, but the manner in which it is argued.

- It helps if you know as much about the other person's attitudes as possible. That way you can tailor your argument to fit the listener.

- Try to disagree as little as possible. Do not argue every little point. If the other person feels that you agree on most things, they are more likely to be persuaded to side with you.

- Choose your timing carefully. Make appointments to see people, or catch them when you know they have time to discuss the matter at length if that is likely to be necessary.

Exercise 20

CARE COSMETICS

Write a brief script (in the first person) that you could use to obtain sales information from branch managers on an individual face-to-face basis. For example, *"Thanks for coming in, Mike – I can see you have some results with you, so let's look at what we need from those..."* etc...

....

....

....

....

....

....

....

....

....

....

....

....

....

....

....

....

....

....

....

....

....

....

....

....

....

....

....

....

....

....

....

....

....

Written Collection of Information

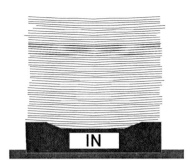

There are various ways in which information may be collected in writing, including:

- Forms – paper-based and online
- Internal mail systems
- Fax
- Email

Paper-based Forms

It seems that whether you are born, die, join a tennis club or enrol in a university, there is always a form to complete for the occasion. Forms can provide an excellent method of collecting information, as long as they are well designed.

A well designed form:

- provides the organisation with ALL information required and does not ask for unnecessary data.

- provides adequate space for details to be written; 1.5 line spacing is satisfactory; double line spacing is preferable.

- has clear instructions and does not confuse the person completing it.

The following example shows a standard form used by a telephone operator to record calls received by an organisation.

Telephone Journal – Care Cosmetics				
Date	Time	Caller	Transferred to:	Other Action/Notes

Example of a form

Examine the following poorly designed form - and the applicant's response.

CARE COSMETICS LTD

APPLICATION FOR GOLD CUSTOMER CLUB MEMBERSHIP

NAME .... *Christina* ....

ADDRESS ...... *14 Heron Street, Brisbane, Queensland* PHONE NO .... *4334 7896* ....

MARITAL STATUS.... *Yes* ...... BIRTHDAY .... *Monday* ....

ARE YOU INTERESTED IN *None of these, I really just want info on hair products* SKIN CARE, MAKEUP, HEALTH FOOD PRODUCTS, OTHER

sun protection and baby care stuff.

Exercise 21

1   What is wrong with the layout of the form?

....

....

2   Where does Christina send this application?

....

3   Can she contact anyone for help?

....

Use Leader Tabs in Forms

There are many computer applications that may be used to create forms. Word is a popular choice, usually using tabs and tables. Leader tabs are particularly useful when a form is created that will be completed in handwriting. The lines created may be dotted, dashed, or solid, depending on the type of leader chosen.

Dots

Name   ....

Dashes

Name   --

Solid

Name   _____

Tip   Use 1.5 or double line spacing with leader tabs to allow space for hand written information.

Exercise 22

1   Launch Word from the All Programs menu on the Start button, or from the icon on your Windows Desktop. If the Task Pane at the right of the Word window is open, close it.

2   Press Ctrl 5 to change the line spacing for the document to 1.5.

3   Type: **Name**

4   Click on the ruler at 1.5 cm to set a left tab.

5   Set a second tab on the ruler as near as possible to the Right Indent indicator (ie the right margin), then click and drag the tab directly onto the right margin.

6   Choose [Format] Tabs.

7   In the Tabs dialog box, click on the tab that has been set at the right margin so that it appears in the Tab stop position: box. (Your tab may appear at a different point on the ruler than illustrated below, depending on margin settings in Word.)

8   Select option 2 from the Leader section.

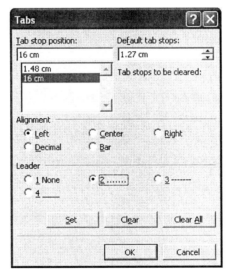

9   Click on OK.

> **Tip**   To adjust settings for more than one tab, in the Tabs dialog box select the first tab to be changed, modify settings as required, click on the Set button (instead of OK), then select the second tab and continue in the same manner. When all changes have been made, click on OK.

10 With the cursor still located at the end of the typed text, press Tab twice.

Name   ....

11 Press Enter and type: **Address**

12 Press Tab twice, then press Enter.

13 Type: **Phone (Home)**

14 On the ruler, drag the tab set at 1.5 cm to 3 cm.

15 Set new tabs at 7 cm, 8 cm and 11 cm by clicking on the ruler.

16 Apply a leader (option 2) to the 7 cm tab, using the Tabs dialog box.

17 With the cursor still located at the end of the typed text, press Tab three times.

18 Type: **Phone (Work)**

19 Press Tab twice.

20 Save your document with the name **Example Form**

[Note]   Ctrl Q will delete all paragraph formatting, including any tabs set.

Exercise 23

In Word, recreate the form on page 31 ensuring it is well laid out, and using leader tabs. Print, save and close your document.

Exercise 24

Using the spreadsheet working plan you created in Exercise 5 for reference, create a form in Word that could be used to collect sales results by telephone from each branch. Print, save and close your document.

Online Forms

Online forms are a very effective way of collecting information, combining the efficiency of forms with the advantages of the Internet. Online forms are most commonly used to collect information from customers; however they also have a place as an internal information collection tool. Many organisations have an Intranet – an internal Internet for use within the company. In many respects, it replaces the need for paper-based information, and a physical internal mail delivery system. The Intranet, as well as being used to *disseminate* information, may also be used to *collect* it.

Online forms can be created in packages such as Word, or in web design packages such as FrontPage or Dreamweaver. Once uploaded to an organisation's Intranet, the form can be completed and submitted online, obviously being reused as frequently and by as many people as needed.

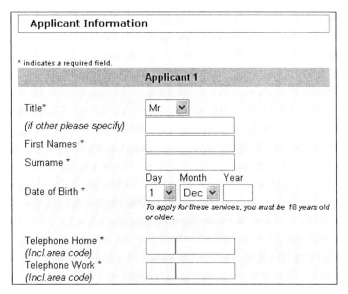

Example of an online form

Internal Mail

Most organisations that employ large numbers of staff will use an internal mail system. Internal mail is basically a form of written communication that has been generated solely for use within an organisation, ie to be read only by staff.

Inter-office mail

Internal mail delivery systems provide for the collection and delivery of memos, reports, and other documents, within an organisation – this could be just within a single site, or across buildings or branches. Mail may be delivered personally, or may be sorted into centrally located pigeon holes for collection. Usually internal mail is sent in resealable envelopes, with the destination name and department written on the front. Inter-office mail avoids the expense and risks of security lapses that are inherent when using external mail delivery systems.

This system can be invaluable where there are several large departments requiring a good communication link.

Memoranda (memos)

Memos are used as reminders, confirmation of events, or information providers to other staff members. An example is shown below.

Acceptable memo formats vary, but should include:

- Name of the writer
- Name of the intended recipient
- Date
- Subject
- Message

Sometimes a file reference is also included.

A memo can be sent to a group of people or to individuals. If sent to a group, then a copy is usually sent to each person. If a memo is to be viewed by everyone, it can be pinned on an office notice board.

MEMO	
To	All staff
From	Henry Simpson, Stationery Requisitions
Date	4 October 2002
Subject	October stationery order

I will be away on annual leave from 18 - 22 October. This means that the stationery order for October will have to be processed one week earlier than usual.

Please forward your requests to me by Wednesday, 13 October at the latest.

Example of a Memo

Exercise 25

Use Word to prepare a memo to branch managers requesting the sales information required in the scenario at the beginning of the book. Print, save and close the document.

Circulation slips

Typically attached to the front of a journal, magazine, book, newsletter or other document, a circulation slip notes the names of interested individuals. In this way the slip is used to pass information from one person/department to another. As each interested party finishes with the document, s/he crosses her/his name off the list and sends the document, through the internal mail, to the next name on the circulation slip.

Fax

Collecting information by fax can be very effective. Information is transmitted in scanned form via telephone lines. It is not necessary for the sender to have computer or keyboard skills in order to use a fax. Standard forms used for information collection can be used effectively if responses are received by fax.

The cost of sending many faxes may be unnecessary if email can do the same job – particularly if faxes are sent to toll calling areas, as email messages do not incur a toll call cost.

Email

Email can be used extensively to communicate with others within the office (for example the telephonist may use it to relay telephone and visitor messages) and also as an efficient means of communicating with staff in other offices (in this country or abroad), as well as with clients and suppliers. The versatility, speed, low cost and efficiency of email has seen it become one of the most popular methods of written communication used in organisations over the past few years. It provides an excellent means by which to collect information, offering:

- a written record of information, reducing the likelihood of errors;

- a non-intrusive approach – people can read and send information at a time convenient to them;

- savings in time, avoiding the general niceties that take up time in a face-to-face meeting or phone conversation;

- an efficient way to collect the same information from several people, as a message can be sent once but to several people;

- a cost-effective option when information is being collected from a distance, as the cost of toll calls is avoided;

- a resource-efficient option; in offices that are served by a computer network, sending an email does not tie up a phone line, whereas making a phone call or sending a fax will do.

Microsoft Outlook is a desktop organiser that includes an email facility, allowing email messages to be sent and received. Outlook provides a means of recording, storing and sorting appointment details, tasks, and contact names and addresses. Outlook can also be used to keep track of activities.

Exercise 26

➢ Launch Outlook from the All Programs menu on the Start button, or from the icon on your desktop.

Outlook Bar

Features in Microsoft Outlook can be accessed from the Outlook Bar as shown below.

The Outlook Bar displays shortcuts to Outlook options. These are accessed by clicking on the relevant shortcut, eg when you click on Contacts, the content of Contacts appears in the Information Viewer.

Outlook Today	**Outlook Today**	Provides a view of your day, appointments, tasks and any email messages received.
Inbox	**Inbox**	Incoming messages are delivered to the Inbox where you can read, reply to and delete them. New messages are created in the Inbox.
Calendar	**Calendar**	A Calendar, Scheduler and TaskPad provide time management tools.
Contacts	**Contacts**	Names and addresses of contacts can be stored and used in conjunction with the email facility.
Tasks	**Tasks**	Tasks may be prioritised, assigned to others as appropriate, and progress on them tracked.
Notes	**Notes**	An electronic version of "post it" notes.
Deleted Items	**Deleted Items**	Any tasks, messages, journal entries, etc that have been deleted in Outlook will appear in Deleted Items.
My Shortcuts	**Displays additional icons:**	Drafts Outbox Sent Items Journal Outlook Update
Other Shortcuts	**Displays additional icons:**	My Computer My Documents Favorites

In this book, the focus will be on the use of the email facility to manage information effectively.

Outlook Window

Exercise 27

➢ Click on Inbox on the Outlook Bar.

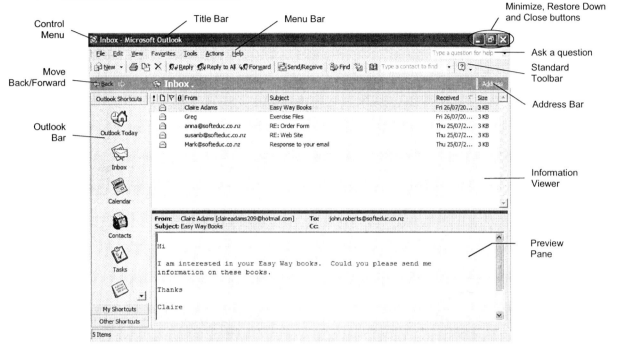

Standard Toolbar

A toolbar that provides quick access to Outlook commands. This toolbar changes depending on the chosen shortcut, eg if you click on Contacts, the toolbar will change to reflect options relating to Contacts (adding a contact, printing, deleting, sending a message, etc).

Information Viewer

The Information Viewer displays any new or current messages received, contacts, tasks etc. This area of the window will change depending on the option selected from the Outlook Bar.

Menu Bar, Title Bar

The Menu bar is used to access Outlook commands. The Title bar displays the program name and the name of the option currently displayed in Outlook.

Minimize, Maximize, Restore Down and Close buttons

These buttons are used to reduce the main window to a button (minimise) on the Taskbar and increase (maximise) the size of the main window (Outlook). When the window is maximised, the Maximize button will display as the Restore Down button. The Close button is used to close Outlook.

Control Menu

The Control Menu can be used to minimise, maximise or close Outlook.

Ask a Question

A Help feature that provides information about Outlook based on questions entered.

Elements in the Outlook Window

When using Microsoft Outlook you can turn on/off (ie display or hide) different elements of the Outlook window, such as the Outlook Bar, Folder List and Preview Pane.

Outlook Bar

➢   To turn on/off choose [View] Outlook Bar.

Folder List

This lists folders set up in Outlook in which you can store and organise information.

➢   To turn on/off choose [View] Folder List.

Preview Pane

When a message is selected in the Inbox, the Preview Pane displays the message contents.

➢   To turn on/off choose [View] Preview Pane.

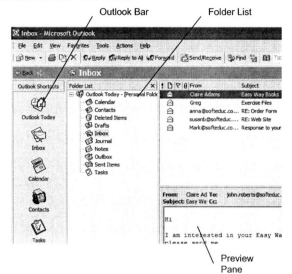

Inbox

Incoming email messages are delivered to the Inbox where you can read, reply to and delete them. New messages are created in and sent from the Inbox.

Exercise 28

Ctrl
Shift I

1   Click on **Inbox** on the Outlook Bar OR click on **Inbox** at the Outlook Today window OR choose [View] Go To, Inbox.

2   Ensure that the Preview Pane is displayed and the Folder List turned off. Use the notes above to help you.

Set up Email Message Format

Exercise 29

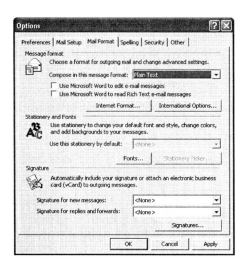

In this book you will send messages in Plain Text format.
Ensure your Outlook settings are as follows, so that they
match the exercise instructions.

1   Choose [Tools] Options. Click on the Mail Format tab.

2   Ensure a tick does <u>not</u> appear in the *Use Microsoft
     Word to edit e-mail messages* and/or *Use Microsoft
     Word to read Rich Text e-mail messages* check boxes.

3   Click on the *Compose in this message format:* ▼ and
     select Plain Text.

4   Click on OK.

When Microsoft Word is set as the email message editor, the window shown below is used to
create new messages, and Word functions are available.

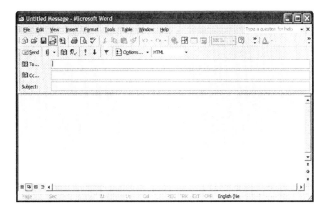

If Outlook is used as the email message editor (as has just been set up in Exercise 29), the window
in which new messages are created is displayed as follows.

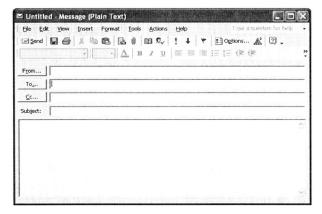

Note   Sending email messages in Plain Text format provides a degree of security to message
         recipients; viruses can attach themselves to Rich Text formats (which occur when Word is
         used as the message editor), but cannot attach to Plain Text format.

         At the end of this section if you wish to revert to using Microsoft Word as your email
         message editor, use the instructions in Exercise 29, placing a tick in the *Use Microsoft
         Word to edit e-mail messages* check box.

Create a New Message

Exercise 30

Ctrl N   1   Click on ⌨ New ▾ OR choose [Actions] New Mail Message OR choose [File] New, Mail Message.

Note   In Outlook 2002, toolbars become personalised automatically as the program is used. This means that the most commonly-used toolbar buttons will display on your toolbar and the display will change as you use Outlook. If the toolbars on your screen do not appear as they are in the screen shot below, make the appropriate following changes until your screen matches the one below.

- Choose [View] Toolbars and ensure there is a tick next to both Standard and Formatting.

- Choose [View] and ensure that the options selected match the options shown at the right.

- Choose [Tools] Customize and click on the Options tab. Click in the *Show Standard and Formatting toolbars on two rows* check box to add a tick, then click on Close.

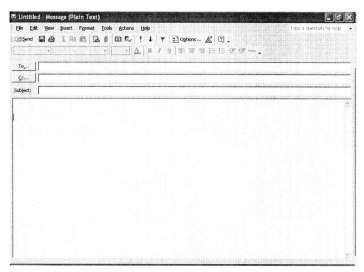

2   Enter the following email address in the To field.

ann.answer@softeduc.co.nz

Always double check that the email address you have entered is spelt correctly.

This message will be sent to Ann Answer (*ann.answer*) at Software Educational (*softeduc*), a company (.*co*) in New Zealand (.*nz*). An automated reply will be sent to you indicating that the message has been received.

3   Press Tab twice to position the cursor in the Subject: field OR click in the Subject: field, then type: **Sending Email**

4   Press Tab OR click in the message area, then type the text exactly as shown below (including the deliberate spelling error).

The Internet is great for transmiting messages to people across the world. I am presently sending an email message. Please send me a reply.

5   Press Enter three times to move down the message window.

6   Type your name.

Set a Priority

Exercise 31

The priority of an email message can be indicated to the recipient as follows.

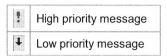

| ! | High priority message |
| ↓ | Low priority message |

1　Click on the Importance: High button ![]. The message will arrive in the recipient's Inbox displaying a high priority indicator. Click on the button again to remove the priority setting.

2　Click on the Importance: Low button ↓. The message will arrive in the recipient's Inbox displaying a low priority indicator. Click on the button again to remove the priority setting.

Spell Check a Message

Exercise 32

F7　1　Choose [Tools] Spelling. Outlook will automatically spell check the message you have written and will highlight potential spelling errors.

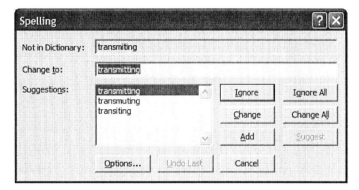

The Not in Dictionary: box displays the incorrect word. The Change to: box displays the most likely alternative. The Suggestions: box lists other alternatives.

2　In this case the correct word is displayed in the Change to: box. Click on Change .

If you do not want to alter the word in the Not in Dictionary: box, click on Ignore. The spell checker will then move on to the next word.

If the word is correct (eg a name) and is frequently used, you may wish to click on Add to add the word to the dictionary. This will prevent the word displaying as an error when it is spell checked in subsequent email messages.

The Change All button changes all occurrences of the incorrect word to the word chosen in the Change to: box, throughout the current email message. The Ignore All button will disregard the word throughout the current message.

When the entire message has been checked the following dialog box will appear.

3　Click on OK.

Send a Message

Exercise 33

1   Click on ⌐ Send .

2   Click on ⌐ Send/Receive to ensure that the message is sent immediately (and to check for any new incoming messages). When a message is sent, a copy of the message appears in the Sent Items folder.

Note   If you are using a dial-up connection to the Internet, clicking on the Send/Receive button will dial your Internet service provider (if you are not already connected). Note that clicking on the Send button alone may not necessarily send your email immediately, so always click on the Send/Receive button to ensure that the message is sent.

Tip   To ensure that all new messages are free of spelling mistakes, choose [Tools] Options, click on the Spelling tab and check the *Always check spelling before sending* option. Click on OK. In future, when you click on the Send button, Outlook will automatically spell check your message before sending it.

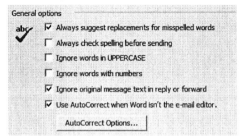

Send a Message to Several People

1   Click on ⌐ New .

2   Type the email address of the first person who is to receive the email in the To field.

Tip   If the email address is entered in the address book (Contacts), you can click on ⌐ To... and select the address required from the Name list.

3   With the cursor located at the end of the first email address, type a semi-colon then add the next email address. Continue in this manner, adding a semi-colon between each address.

4   Click in the Subject: field and type the subject of the message.

5   Click in the message area and type the content.

6   Spell check your message.

7   Click on ⌐ Send , then on ⌐ Send/Receive .

Tip   A distribution list can be created for use when messages are frequently sent to the same group of email addresses (see page 46).

Send a Copy of a Message

1   Click on ⌐ New .

2   In the To field, enter the email address of the person who is to receive the message.

3   Click in the Cc field and enter the email address of the person to whom a copy of the message will be sent.

4   Complete and send your message in the usual manner.

The recipient of the copy will receive the message in their Inbox with their name/email address displayed in the Cc field.

Send a Blind Copy of a Message

At times you may wish to send a copy of a message to someone without other recipients being aware that this has happened. This is known as a blind copy.

1 Click on New. Choose [View] Bcc Field.

2 Enter email addresses in the To and Cc fields in the usual manner.

3 Enter the address of the recipient of the blind copy in the Bcc field, or click on the Bcc... button and select the address if it is in the address book (Contacts).

4 Complete and send your message in the usual manner.

Save a Draft

Saving a draft copy of an incomplete message allows you to return to complete and send it at another time.

1 In an incomplete message, click on the Save button OR choose [File] Save.

2 Choose [File] Close. The message will be saved in the Drafts folder.

3 Choose [View] Folder List. Select the Drafts folder to view the incomplete message. Your message will appear at the right of the window.

4 Double click on the message to open it. Complete/edit and send your message in the usual manner.

Read a Message

Exercise 34

➢ Click on Send/Receive to check for message delivery. A variety of icons are used to describe the status of messages in the Inbox.

Email Icons

Icon	Description
	Message that has been opened (read)
	Message that has not been opened (unread)
	A file is attached to the message
	A digitally signed message, which has been read
!	High priority message
↓	Low priority message
	Message flagged for follow up
	Message replied to
	Message forwarded

Exercise 35

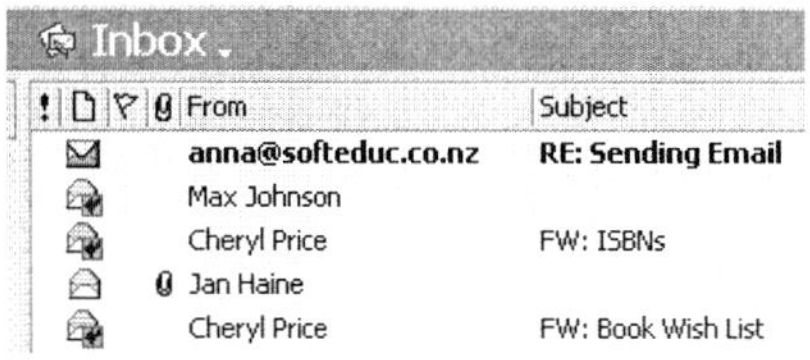

Messages received will be displayed in the Inbox.

To read the reply received from Ann Answer:

1 Click on the message to see the contents displayed in the Preview Pane OR double click on the message to open it in a separate window.

2 Read the message, then, if the message is displayed in a window, click on Close OR choose [File] Close

Print a Message

Exercise 36

1   Click on the message received from Ann Answer if it is not already selected.

Ctrl P 2   Choose [File] Print, select the printer, ensure Memo Style is selected and click on OK

    OR

    Click on the Print button .

Reply to a Message

Exercise 37

1   Click on the message received from Ann Answer if it is not already selected.

Ctrl R 2   Click on   Reply

    OR

    Choose [Actions] Reply.

    The subject field content from the received message is copied into the Subject field of the new message, preceded by RE:

3   With the cursor in the Message area above the `-----Original Message-----` banner, type: **Thank you for your email.**

4   Send the message in the usual manner.

Reply to All Recipients of a Message

At times you may receive a message that has been sent to several recipients. If you would like to send your reply to all of them, do the following.

Ctrl Shift R 1   Click on   Reply to All OR choose [Actions] Reply to All.

2   Complete and send your message in the usual manner.

Reply to a Message without displaying the Original Message

Ctrl R 1   Click on the message to which you wish to reply, then click on   Reply OR choose [Actions] Reply.

2   Click in the Subject: field and delete RE:

3   Select the text from `-----Original Message-----` to the end of the message. Press Delete. The email address of the person who sent the message to which you are replying will still appear in the To field.

4   Enter and send your message in the usual manner.

 Outlook settings can be changed so that the original message is never included in your reply. Choose [Tools] Options. From the Preferences tab click on the E-mail Options button. In the On replies and forwards section, click on the When replying to a message and select Do not include original message. Click on OK, then on OK again.

Forward a Message

Ctrl F   1   Click on the email reply from Ann Answer. Click on **Forward** OR choose [Actions] Forward.

2   In the To field, enter the email address of the person to whom you wish to forward the message: **susan.brown@softeduc.co.nz**.

3   Click in the body of the message and add the following text above the ----Original Message---- banner.

Hi Susan

You can practise sending email messages to ann.answer@softeduc.co.nz.

(Your name)

4   Send the message in the usual manner.

Delete a Message

1   Click on the message from Ann Answer if it is not already selected.

2   Press the Delete key OR click on the Delete button ✕.

The message will be transferred to the Deleted Items folder. (If you wish to permanently delete a message, display the Deleted Items folder, select the message, press the Delete key and click on Yes to confirm.)

Tip   To permanently delete a message directly from the Inbox, select the message then hold down the Shift key and press Delete. Click on Yes to confirm that you wish to permanently delete the message. (The message will <u>not</u> be sent to the Deleted Items folder.)

Select Messages

By selecting messages you can perform an action on several messages at once, eg you could delete or print several messages at one time, or you could move a group of messages to another folder.

Methods of selecting messages are described below.

Selection	Action
Single message	Click on the message.
List of messages	Click on the first message. Hold down the Shift key and click on the last message.
Random messages	Click on the first message to be selected. Hold down the Ctrl key and click on each message you wish to select. If you select the wrong message, hold down the Ctrl key and click on the message again to deselect it.

Create a Distribution List

A distribution list is a group of email addresses to which you frequently send the same message. Instead of entering each individual email address on every occasion, you can assign a name to the entire group and just send the message to that group's name.

1   Click on Contacts on the Outlook Bar.

^{Ctrl}
^{Shift L}   2   Click on the New button ▾ and select Distribution List OR choose [Actions] New Distribution List OR choose [File] New, Distribution List.

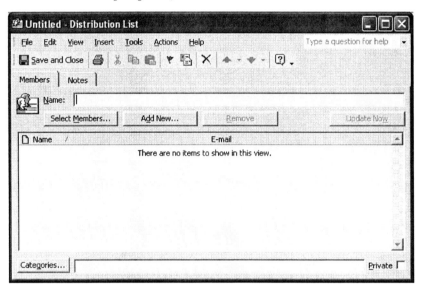

3   In the Name: box enter a name for the distribution list, eg All Staff Members.

4   Click on Select Members... .

5   From the Name section of the Select Members dialog box, click on the name of a person to be added to the distribution list. Click on Members -> to copy the name to the Add to distribution list: box. Repeat for each individual to be added.

6   Click on OK when finished. The names and email addresses of all members of the distribution list will be displayed.

> **Notes**   •   To remove an individual from the list, select the name and click on Remove .
>
>   •   Click on Add New... to add a new person to the list whose details are not already held in the address book (Contacts). Enter the information for the new member. If you wish to add the person to Contacts, click in the *Add to Contacts* check box. Click on OK.

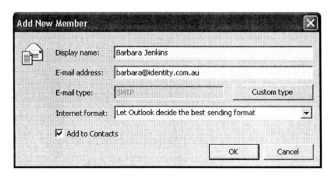

7   Click on ![Save and Close].

The distribution list will be displayed in the Contacts window.

All Staff Members

Notes   •   To edit the distribution list double click on it in Contacts.

•   To use the distribution list click on the To button in a new message, and select the distribution list instead of an individual contact, then proceed in the usual manner.

•   In the lists of Contacts, indicates that the name is of a distribution list, rather than an individual.

Exercise 40

Create an entry in Contacts for Ann Answer as follows.

1   Click on ![Contacts] on the Outlook bar (if you are not already in Contacts).

2   Click on ![New].

3   Complete details in the Untitled – Contact dialog box as shown below.

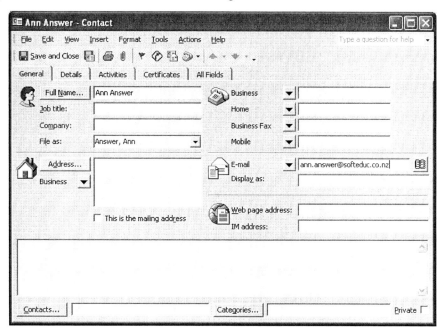

4   Click on ![Save and Close].

Note   Contacts will automatically suggest filing your contact by surname first, in the File as: box.

Exercise 41

1   Create a contact for Susan Brown; her email address is: **susan.brown@softeduc.co.nz**

2   Create a distribution list named **Software Education** for Ann Answer and Susan Brown.

3   Compose and send a new email message to the Software Education distribution list. The subject of the message should read: **Staff Meeting**

The body of the message should read: **Please attend a staff meeting next Monday in the staff room at 10 am.**

Attach Files to a Message

Files can be attached to an email message as an alternative to printing them and posting or faxing the document.

Exercise 42

1   Create a message to **susan.brown@softeduc.co.nz**. The subject of the message is: **Books**. Advise that you are attaching information on Learning Series and Easy Way books.

2   Click on the Insert File button ![paperclip] OR choose [Insert] File.

3   Locate and select the Word file named **Book Description**, from My Documents folder.

(Your list of files will differ from those shown below.)

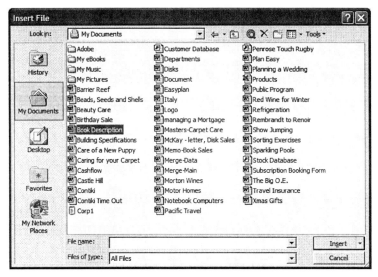

4   Click on [Insert ▾].

An Attach field will be displayed in the email message, containing details of the attached file.

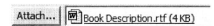

5   Send the message in the usual manner.

[Note]   When a message is <u>received</u> with an attachment, a paper clip icon is displayed next to the message header in the Inbox, eg ✉ ◊ Claire Adams

Double click on the attachment in an open message to open the attached file.

Save an Attachment received in a Message

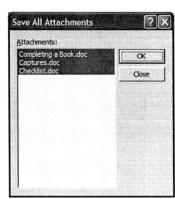

1   Open the email message containing the attachment.

2   Choose [File] Save Attachments.

[Note]   If there is more than one file the Save All Attachments dialog box appears. By default all files will be selected. You can select and deselect files in the usual manner. Click on OK to save the selected files.

3   Use the Look in: ▼ to locate and select the folder in which the attachment(s) will be saved (if there is only one attachment to save, the box will be called the Save in: box).

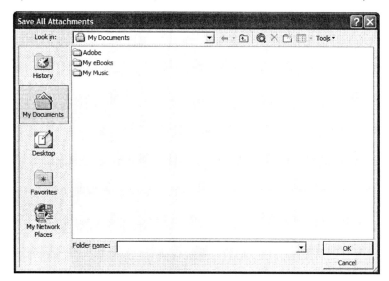

4   Click on OK (or Save, if there is only one attachment).

Flag a Message

After a message has been read, you may wish to flag it to indicate that follow up is needed.

Exercise 43

1   Double click on the reply from Susan Brown (RE: Books) in the Inbox.

Ctrl
Shift G   2   Click on the Follow Up button ⚑.

3   Ensure Follow up is selected in the Flag to: box.

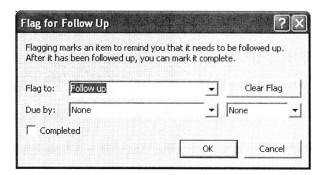

4   Click on the Due by: ▼ and select tomorrow's date.

5   Click on OK. Choose [File] Close to close the message.

6   Flag icons are displayed next to flagged message in the Inbox. To view the flag status of all messages in the Inbox, choose [View] Current View, By Follow-up Flag.

7   To return to the previous view of the Inbox, choose [View] Current View, Messages.

Which Collection Method is Best?

The decision on the best method to use to collect information should be based around the following questions.

- How frequently does the information need to be collected?

  Daily? Weekly? Monthly? Is there some other timeframe that is more relevant?

- How complex is the information?

  If the information is factual and simple, a written collection method may be most efficient, but if discussion is required or information may require explaining, a more direct method may be better.

- How confidential is the information?

  If confidentiality is important, security issues surrounding some collection methods, such as email and mobile phones, should be considered.

- Is the volume of information to be collected at any one time small or large?

  While a few figures may be easily provided as part of an email message, it would be more efficient to collect a larger amount of data in a format where re-entering of data is not required.

- From whom will the information be collected?

  Are you collecting information from people in your office, branch offices in other parts of the country or overseas? Is the cost of toll calls a consideration in deciding the best collection method?

Exercise 44

 Decide on the most efficient way to collect the sales information needed for Care Cosmetics. Consider the following issues.

1   How would you explain to branch managers what information is needed, and get their "buy in"? (The topics covered in pages 10-29 will provide you with some clues!)

   ....
   ....
   ....
   ....
   ....

2   What on-going method of collection would you use and why?

   ....
   ....
   ....
   ....
   ....

Sources of Information

Sometimes, knowing the method by which you will collect information is not enough – you may need to complete some research to source the information you need. The following ideas will help you to find information on a huge range of topics.

The Internet

The Internet is probably the best source of information, and the most up to date. However, you do need to acquire some "surfing" skills in order to be able to sort out the relevant from the irrelevant! Surfing the Internet can take a long time as there is so much interesting information available, and it is very easy to get side-tracked.

There are a number of excellent Search Engines, which will search for keywords, and group information for you. Different search engines tend to produce better results in different areas, and most people use a few favourites that reflect the type of information they most usually source. Some to try are:

- www.google.com
- www.dogpile.com
- www.altavista.com

Books

You will need to refer to books for technical or specific information (eg computing, engineering, science, law, commerce, phone books, maps), but make sure that the information is up to date. Computing books, in particular, become outdated very rapidly.

Newspapers

Available online and in printed form, most newspapers are indexed and are also in sections, making it easy for readers to go straight to the topics in which they are interested. Local papers are useful for advertisements for local jobs and local tradespeople.

TV

The news and current affairs programmes are a very good source of information, but the interpretation of information is sometimes debatable, and may depend on the reputation of the reporter(s).

People

Listen to "experts", but do your own research also. Use your own judgement – sometimes people who have the most to say have the least reason to say it.

Radio

News and current affairs programmes will keep you informed of what is happening in the world. Other programmes (music, health, sports, etc) will keep you up to date with developments in areas in which you may have a special interest. Note: Talkback shows are often patronised by isolated individuals with a chip on their shoulder – listen to these for entertainment, not for education!

Magazines and Journals

There are a number of excellent publications which provide in-depth information on a huge range of topics, eg PC World, Time, and National Geographic. Many of these publications also have an Internet presence.

Attending Courses

Do your own research before enrolling – compare a number of courses (price, length, tutor qualifications, outcomes, reputation, etc). Ask for a course outline before you enrol. Check the local and national papers, phone books, yellow pages, Chamber of Commerce directories, and the Internet for listings.

Libraries

Many libraries offer Internet access, information on microfiche, and excellent reference sections. Ask the librarians for assistance.

Agencies

City councils, Citizens Advice Bureaux, professional societies – all have a range of information, resources and contacts to help you search for the information you need.

Exercise 45

Where would you look for the following information?

1   A weather report for tomorrow for Sydney ....

2   A local, part-time job ....

3   Breaking news stories ....

4   Current investment interest rates ....

5   Bed and breakfast accommodation in Dublin..

6   The latest Microsoft products ....

Meet Organisational Requirements

Different organisations have different requirements for the collection of information. Some requirements are common to all, because they are a matter of legislation. An example of this would be the need for information collected about individuals (staff, clients, or others) to be completed in compliance with the Privacy Amendment (Private Sector) Act 2000.

The requirements of an organisation will usually be found in various forms of documentation, which may be collected together into a Policy and Procedures manual. A manual of this type could extend across several volumes and typically contains information on:

Excerpts from Care Cosmetics' Human Resources Policy and Procedure manual

- Human resources – position descriptions, organisational structures, employment, code of ethics, remuneration, training.

- Health and Safety – legal requirements, procedures relating to the way in which work is completed.

- Documentation standards – logos, standard forms and templates.

- Quality Assurance – documentation of standards required, how these are maintained and details of any accreditation in this area.

- Products – information about the products/services that are provided by the organisation.

- Security – keys, combinations, passwords, and procedures regarding access levels and the safety of buildings and information.

- Purchasing – recommended suppliers, purchasing procedures and authority.

- Customer service – minimum standards, key account handling and complaints handling.

Most organisations will have internal procedures in place for the handling of information, particularly in terms of confidentiality issues surrounding commercially sensitive information, such as the sales results used in the Care Cosmetics scenario.

Some of these issues are discussed in the topics that follow.

An Example of an Information Collection Procedure

As part of their security procedures, many large firms keep a reception register which provides a permanent record of every visitor to the firm, and who they are visiting.

A reception register should contain the following information:

- Date
- Name of visitor
- Name of visitor's company
- Name of staff member being visited
- Car registration number
- Time in
- Time out

For example:

DATE	NAME	COMPANY	STAFF CONTACT	CAR REG. NO.	TIME IN	TIME OUT

In some instances the visitor will also be provided with a security tag to wear at all times while on the premises. This will identify him/her as an approved visitor.

There are several reasons for this screening, including:

- Maintenance of building and information security
- Safety of both staff and visitors
- Prevention of unauthorised entry
- Legal requirements surrounding safety issues

Standardised Documentation

Most large organisations have requirements about how (for example) notes should be taken, transcribed, formatted and stored and how documents should be created and presented. These requirements are referred to as "house style". House styles are used by organisations in which presentation is regarded as very important, such as publishing companies, advertising agencies, and design companies. House styles are used because:

- If a standard, pre-designed format is used, it is more likely that all the required information will be included. It is easy to forget important details when confronted with a blank piece of paper.
- Standard layouts become familiar to employees. People know exactly where to look for the piece of information they need and might not need to read through an entire document to find what they require.
- Standard formats tend to look neater and more professional.
- Standard formats save time – the author of the document does not need to work out how to lay out and format their work.

An organisation could have requirements for any of the following.

- Presentation of documents – eg all documents in a particular font (typically Arial or Times New Roman).

- Use of a style guide which outlines the rules adopted by the organisation for the production of documents. This may incorporate all of the items in this list, and others.

- Storage and naming of documents – eg documents may need to be saved to a specific part of the computer network, and named using particular conventions.

- Consistency of phrases – for example, some companies never use the word "we" in outside correspondence.

- Use of templates – the organisation may have letter, fax cover sheet and memo templates which must always be used. This saves time for the author of the documents and also ensures consistency across the organisation.

- Use of logos – there may be specific logos that must be used with different types of documents, and there may be rules regarding changing the size or proportion of logos.

Standard Formats

The standardisation of documents helps to create an image/brand for an organisation. Documents may include:

- Letterhead
- Memos
- Faxes
- Agendas
- Minutes of Meetings
- Email messages
- Reports
- Spreadsheets (headings and formatting)
- Balance sheets and accounting documents, eg invoices, statements
- Additional documents relating to the type of business, eg in a legal firm this would include wills, deeds etc.

Templates

A template is a read-only file that contains all the permanent text and formatting required to form the basis of a new document of a specific type. The variable information is the only remaining data entry requirement. Templates are used for documents that are created often, eg a Word fax form, Excel balance sheet, product launch PowerPoint presentation etc.

Templates are usually set up by staff experienced in creating the end documents and in the software program. The templates can then be used easily by other staff who do not have such strong technology skills or knowledge of the business.

Styles

A style is a set of formatting instructions combined into a meaningful name that can be applied easily to text, eg formatting instructions for a heading that is Arial, 14 pt, left aligned and bold, could be assigned as **Heading 1**.

The following documents show examples of organisational style requirements of formatting for Software Publications Pty Ltd. Notice the same company logo, colour scheme, templates, etc are used throughout.

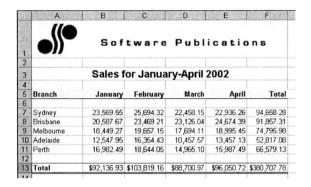

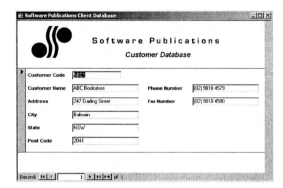

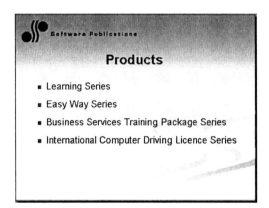

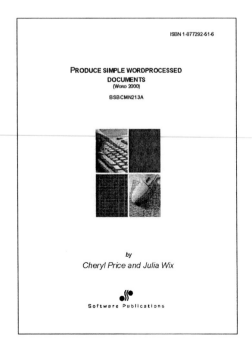

Exercise 46

Consider the informal manner in which sales information is currently handled at Care Cosmetics. Decide whether or not it is likely that the following organisational requirements of the firm are being met, and comment on why in each case.

1   Accuracy and overall quality of the information.

....
....
....
....
....
....
....
....
....
....

2   Compliance with appropriate legislation.

....
....
....
....
....
....
....
....
....
....

3   Standardised documentation.

....
....
....
....
....
....
....
....
....
....

Organise Information

Learning Outcomes

At the end of this section you should be able to -

☐   Collate information in a logical manner.

☐   Maintain information security standards to meet organisational requirements.

☐   Use business equipment and technology to maintain information.

☐   Organise information in a suitable format for analysis, interpretation and dissemination.

Introduction

In this section you will learn how to manage information after it has been collected. This will involve organising the information to make it usable, understanding information security requirements, and learning about the business equipment and technology that can be used to help manage information.

Collate Information

Collating means putting into order or organising. This can range from ensuring that two associated pieces of paper are attached to each other, to organising 20 sets of papers into separate piles. When the term 'collating' is used in this particular business context it means taking the information that has been received and placing it with any associated paperwork or files.

Many organisations deal regularly with the same people. As information arrives into their offices it can be identified and linked up to the relevant background information.

In a large business, collating can mean sorting information received into department order so that it can be sent to the correct place.

The following steps illustrate one method of ensuring that relevant information is collected and arranged logically.

Select Relevant Information

1   Identify the problem; ie write down the topic and the questions to be answered.

2   Decide on the information source(s) and methods to be used, eg the Internet, phone calls to suppliers of mobile phones, etc.

3   Gather the information together (brochures, printouts, photocopies, written pages, etc).

4   Keep all the information in a labelled file box so that you won't misplace it.

5   Sort through the information and discard or cross out any information that is irrelevant or repeated elsewhere.

Arrange Information in a Logical Sequence

1   Sort the collected information by topic. You may find that you have gathered far too much information on one topic, but not enough on another. If necessary, staple each set of information together, and mark each printout with a one or two-word topic heading.

2   Review your topic list, and sort each set of information into order, depending on which question it answers, eg 1, 2, 3, 4. Number them accordingly.

3   Use the Outline function of a word processing program to type the topic headings. Apply the appropriate heading levels – you will learn how to do this on pages 62 to 65. You may then decide to return to Normal or Page/Print Layout to enter information under the headings. Save your document with an appropriate name.

4   If required, add a list of reference sources.

5   Number the pages.

6   Create a Table of Contents (you will learn how to do this on pages 65 and 66).

7   Create a title page containing the name of the topic you have researched, your name and the date.

Note If writing a list of instructions ensure you include each step – never assume the person following the instructions should automatically know something. Make sure the instructions are in logical sequence. Read through the list. Follow the instructions yourself (a "walk-through") and adjust if necessary.

Organise Information in Word

Word has several tools designed to assist in organising information. Some of these, such as Outlining and Table of Contents, are mentioned in the topic *Collate Information* on this and the previous pages. In this part of Section 2, you will gain an overview of these tools.

Outlines

An Outline enables you to see the overall view of a Word document. It is useful when moving large amounts of text to restructure a very long document, and when sorting information into a logical order. It is necessary to have an understanding of Styles before using the Outline function.

Understand Styles

A style is a set of formatting instructions assigned to a name so that it can be applied easily to text. For example, formatting instructions for a heading that is Arial, 14 pt, left aligned and bold, could be named **Heading 1**. Styles can be created, modified and deleted from the Styles and Formatting Task Pane, and may be assigned to shortcut keys for efficiency.

When in Normal View, a "Styles Bar" can be displayed. Names of styles applied will appear at the left of document text.

Styles provide consistency and save time; when a style is edited all occurrences of that style will change throughout the document. Styles also form the basis of a Table of Contents.

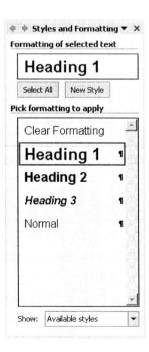

There are a number of different style types in Word 2002 – character, paragraph, table, and list style formatting. In this book you will learn how to apply paragraph styles.

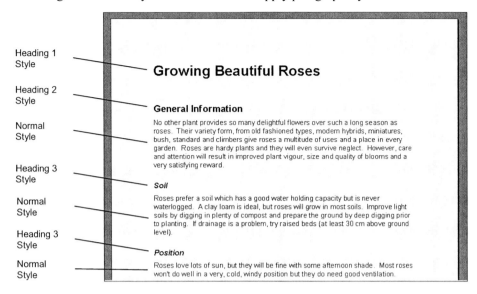

In the above document the following paragraph styles have been used.

Heading 1	Arial 24 pt, bold, left aligned, 12 pt spacing before
Heading 2	Arial 16 pt, bold, left aligned, 12 pt spacing before, 6 pt spacing after
Heading 3	Arial 13 pt, bold, italic, left aligned, 6 pt spacing before, 6 pt spacing after
Normal	Arial 12 pt, left aligned

Apply Styles

Exercise 47

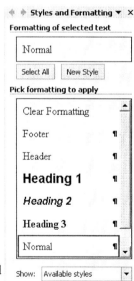

1   Launch Word.

2   Open the file named **Care of a New Puppy**. The Normal style for this document is Times New Roman 12 pt.

3   Click on the Styles and Formatting button 🖍 on the Formatting toolbar.

4   From the Styles and Formatting Task Pane click on the Show: ▾ and select Available styles.

5   With the cursor in the heading Care of a New Puppy, click on Heading 1 in the *Pick formatting to apply* box in the Styles and Formatting Task Pane.

6   Position the mouse pointer over the Heading 1 style in the Styles and Formatting Task Pane to see a description of the formatting used in the style.

7   Click the cursor in the next heading, Going Home, on the same page, and choose Heading 2 style. Apply Heading 2 style to the remaining side headings until you reach the heading Vaccination (you can use F4 to repeat styles).

8   Click the cursor in the heading Vaccination. Styles can also be applied from the Formatting toolbar. Click on the Style ˅ on the Formatting toolbar and select Heading 3.

The Style box on the Formatting toolbar not only displays information about a style but also about formatting applied to the current paragraph. What appears in the Style box will depend on the option chosen in the Show: box in the Styles and Formatting Task Pane (eg 'All styles', 'Available styles' etc).

Style

9   Change all remaining subheadings of Health Care to Heading 3, up to and including the heading *Fleas*. Shortcut keys (shown below) can be used to apply styles.

10   To see the style names on your screen, change to Normal View, then choose [Tools] Options, and click on the View tab. Change the measurement in the Style area width: box to 1.5 cm. Click on OK. Scroll down through the document to see the styles you have applied. (The Style box displays the name of the style applied to the paragraph in which the cursor is currently located.)

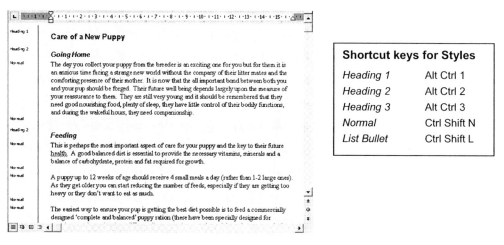

Shortcut keys for Styles	
Heading 1	Alt Ctrl 1
Heading 2	Alt Ctrl 2
Heading 3	Alt Ctrl 3
Normal	Ctrl Shift N
List Bullet	Ctrl Shift L

11   Apply Heading 3 style to the headings Teething and Grooming and Heading 2 style to the heading Registration.

12   Change the Style area width back to 0 cm.

13   Save and close the document.

View an Outline

In the following exercise you will view and learn how to use an outline.

Exercise 48

1   Open the document named **Growing Roses.** Close the Task Pane if it is open. Styles have been used in this document.

2   Click on the Outline View button 🔲 at the bottom left of your screen OR choose [View] Outline.

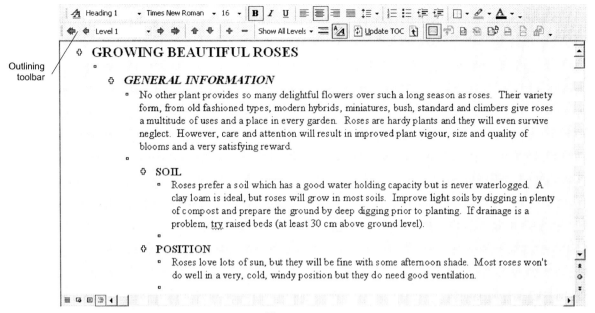

Notice that headings are displayed with a ✛ symbol and body text is denoted by a ▫ symbol.

(A subtraction symbol indicates that there are no subheadings or body text beneath a heading – usually when a non-heading style is used such as Title style).

Outlining Toolbar Summary

The following is a summary of the buttons on the Outlining toolbar that will be used in this exercise.

Button	Function
⇐	Changes the text to Heading 1 Style.
⇐	Promotes the text to the next heading style.
Level 3 ▾	Displays the existing level of the selected heading. Click on the ▾ to apply another style level to the heading.
⇒	Demotes the text one level.
⇒	Demotes the text to body text.
⬆ ⬇	Moves the selected heading and/or body text up or down in the document.
✛ ━	Expands or collapses headings and body text beneath the selected heading.
Show Level 2 ▾	Determines which levels of heading style are displayed in the document. In this example, styles up to and including Level 2 will be displayed.
═	Displays only the first line of body text in a paragraph.
ᴬ_A_	Displays the outline with/without any formatting (toggle button).

View Headings

➤ Click the ˅ on the Show Level toolbar button 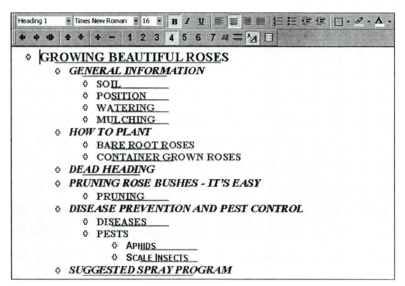 and select Show Level 3.

The thick grey underline indicates that a heading has associated body text or subheadings that are not displayed.

Expand and Collapse Body Text

Exercise 49

1 Click the ˅ on the Show Level toolbar button, and select Show All Levels.

2 To see the outline with no formatting, click on the Show Formatting button ᴬ𝘈 .

3 Click the cursor anywhere in the General Information heading and click on the Collapse button ▬ . All body text beneath the heading will be hidden, but the subheadings will remain displayed.

4 With the cursor in the General Information heading click on the Expand button ✚ to display the body text beneath this heading, and the subheadings.

Promote and Demote Headings

1 Click in the Soil heading and click on the Promote button ⇐ to change the heading to Level 2 style.

2 With the cursor in the Soil heading click on the Demote button ⇒ to change the heading style back to Level 3.

3 Click in the General Information heading and click on the Demote to Body Text button ⇨ .

The symbol ▫ to the left of the heading indicates that it has been changed to body text. Return the heading to the previously applied style by selecting Level 2 from the Outline Level box.

Move Elements of an Outline

1   With the cursor located in the General Information heading, click twice on the Move Down button 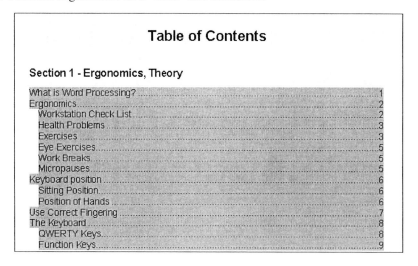. This will move the heading so it is above the Soil heading; the level of the heading remains unchanged.

2   With the cursor in the General Information heading click twice on the Move Up button ⬆ to return the heading to its original place in the document.

3   Click on the ✛ to the left of the Position heading (the cursor changes to a black cross). This selects the heading and any associated subheadings and body text.

4   Click on the Move Up button ⬆ three times – the heading and body text will move together.

5   Alternatively you can move a section by clicking on the ✛ symbol to the left of a heading and drag to move. Try this now to return the Position heading and body text to the original place in the document (a line will appear to guide you).

Headings, subheadings and body text can be demoted or promoted using the ✛ symbol to click and drag to the left or right, however it is usually more accurate to use the Promote and Demote buttons.

6   Click on the ✛ symbol to the left of the Soil heading (the cursor changes to a black cross) then click on the Promote button ⬅.

7   Click on the Demote button ➡ to move the section back again.

When moving elements of an outline it is not necessary to view subheadings and body text as they will automatically be moved when the plus symbol next to the main heading is selected.

8   Close the document without saving the changes.

Table of Contents

A Table of Contents can be found at the front of most books and manuals. It provides a useful reference, as mentioned in the topic *Collate Information*, eliminating the need to sift through an entire collection to find a specific piece of information.

A Table of Contents is generated as a "field" in a document.

A Table of Contents is created in three easy steps.

STEP 1 Apply styles (or mark entries)

STEP 2 Define the format required

STEP 3 Generate the Table of Contents

Create a Table of Contents Based on Heading Styles

Exercise 50

1   Open the file named **Growing Roses**.

2   With the cursor located at the beginning of the document, press Ctrl Enter to create a blank page for the Table of Contents.

3   Press Ctrl Home to move to the top of the blank page, change the style type to Normal, the alignment to left, and type: **Table of Contents**

4   Change the formatting of the heading to Bold, 16 pt, centred. Add 24 pt spacing after the heading.

5   Press End to deselect the heading, then press Enter. Choose [Insert] Reference, Index and Tables, and click on the Table of Contents tab.

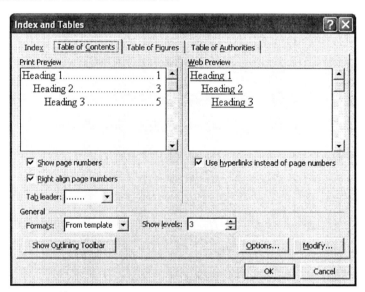

6   Click on the Formats: ▼ and select Classic to determine the format that will be applied to the Table of Contents.

An example of the chosen format is displayed in the Print Preview box. (Web Preview shows how the Table of Contents would be displayed on a web page.)

7   Click on OK to generate the Table of Contents where the cursor is positioned.

8   Save the changes and close the document.

Information Security

The security of information in an organisation needs to be carefully considered in order to meet required legal and ethical standards. This is especially the case when there are many staff involved in the processing of information.

Telephone

In many offices, matters discussed over the telephone may be confidential. In a busy office, this may necessitate having the call transferred to a more private place or having it postponed until privacy can be guaranteed. For example, a conversation about an unpaid bill could have unfortunate repercussions for the client if it was overheard by the wrong person.

Care has to be taken in a home office situation where the phone may be used by the family as well as for the business. Clients will doubt the confidentiality of their calls if they are punctuated by children talking on another extension. If intrusions such as this are likely to occur, then a separate business line should be installed.

Mail

Business mail may include not only orders for goods and services, but also highly confidential and sensitive information. For this reason, it must be handled with considerable care. Recommended methods include:

- collection from the post office in a sealed bag (if not delivered);
- allocation of sorting to specific, trained employees (if not owner operated);
- establishing procedures for dealing with confidential and sensitive material;
- dealing with the mail promptly and efficiently as it arrives;
- ensuring that all mail reaches the appropriate people as quickly as possible;
- ensuring that mail is not left unattended or exposed to the view of the general public.

Faxes

With some fax machines, information arriving will be printed "face up" on the machine paper. In this case the machine should be placed where faxes received will not be exposed to public view. Faxed information received through a computer system is more secure, because access to it is subject to the control of the computer operator.

Email

Email allows users to send and receive messages and documents through a computer system (network). Only authorised people should have access to this particular area of the computer. Email addresses used for general correspondence or for receiving orders should be checked regularly and messages sorted and distributed appropriately as soon as possible. This may mean forwarding messages to relevant people, or printing out messages for distribution through normal paper-based channels.

Email can be read by anyone who has access to the computer on which the message was received. Copies of email messages remain on servers (other computers), may be intercepted en route from the sender to the receiver, and can be monitored. For these reasons, email is not a confidential means of communication, unless special encryption is used to make the content unreadable to anyone who doesn't hold the encryption "key".

Information Sources within an Office

Offices generally contain a vast amount of information. All information should be classified and any highly sensitive material kept in a safe, secure place. If written, it should be kept in folders in a lockable filing cabinet with access limited to approved personnel. Depending on the organisation, customer records, staff records and the business accounting system may belong to this category.

Where records are held in computer files, the computers must be set up to limit access to authorised operators.

Office and Physical Resource Security

Individual offices, as well as the main premises, should be locked if information is sensitive, or if, for example, an office contains equipment such as a network server computer. Cars used as temporary offices by travelling sales representatives should always be locked.

In a large organisation, not all staff will have keys to lock and unlock the main business premises, nor all the office areas within. It will depend on the general security policy of the organisation. Locking and unlocking the main building may be the responsibility of a security guard, who may also monitor traffic in and out during business hours.

Burglar alarms and other security devices are now essential aids in office security because of increased theft and damage to business premises. Many businesses pay a monthly fee to a security company to check their premises and patrol the area each night.

Offices contain many physical resources that need to be made secure and inaccessible to unauthorised people. Most office equipment can now be programmed to restrict access. These include:

- Photocopiers – security cards may be used to activate copiers.
- Computers – passwords can be used to limit access.
- Fax machines – codes may be set up so that faxes are stored and printed only when the code is entered.

Storage and Disposal of Information

The two main methods of storing office information are:

- Physical filing systems
- Computers

There is always a need for a certain amount of information storage within a business situation. For example, customer records have to be retained for reference, and the Australian Taxation Office requires that all accounting documentation be kept for a number of years. In the interests of organisational security, there are usually certain requirements for the way in which information is stored and when and how it should be disposed of.

Filing Systems

All data in any type of filing system should be treated as confidential. Customer records, for example, should be stored in a safe, secure location out of sight of unauthorised personnel.

Filing cabinets should be fireproof and lockable.

File records should never be disposed of without specific approval from an authorised person. Obviously, there will come a time in most businesses when it is impractical to keep all records and there should be specific policies regarding disposal.

Files can be classified according to the way in which they are being used. They go through four main stages during their life cycle as follows.

Active files	Files that are in constant use. These should be kept securely in a convenient location. Examples include the files of those customers who are still making regular purchases from the business.
Semi-active files	These are used occasionally. Examples could include customers who have not made a purchase for a considerable time, but who are still sent mail-outs.
Non-active files	Files that are not really used. However, they contain documents that are being kept in case they are needed. They may include the files of customers who have recently left the area.
Inactive files	These are files that are not needed in any administrative capacity and contain documents that will not be required in the future.

Files should be checked regularly while they are still in use. Any unwanted information can be removed and destroyed, provided the correct authority has been given.

Security in Relation to Information Disposal

Confidential information should not be thrown out with the usual office rubbish as there is a risk that some pages could escape and a breach of confidentiality could occur.

Correct ways of destroying unwanted material include:

- Tearing into small pieces
- Placing through a paper shredding machine
- Burning

All of these methods ensure that unauthorised people cannot view whole documents. There are companies that specialise in document storage and/or disposal, and it may be an organisation's policy to use these professional services for document management.

Computers

Computers have the ability to store vast amounts of information. Information may be stored on a computer's hard drive, on a network drive, or on removable storage media, such as floppy disks, CDs, and tapes.

The security requirements for information stored in a computer system are the same as those for paper files. All data must be considered confidential to the business. Computers have their own filing systems and these can provide easy access to information. Care must be taken to ensure that only authorised people have access to specific information, by the use of passwords.

Files should be retained in logically named folders/directories so that relevant information can be extracted as required. If data is being stored on a hard drive, it is important to remember that it is not safe unless a backup copy is made and kept current. Otherwise, if the computer is damaged or stolen, records could be irretrievable.

When files are stored on disks, they need to be kept locked away in a safe place. Disks can be damaged and/or misplaced if they are not stored correctly. The risk of damage can be reduced if disks are kept away from dust, magnetic fields and heat. Ideally, they should be kept in a specially designed storage box in a fireproof cabinet.

While access to computers can be protected by the use of passwords, it is not possible to restrict access to disks in the same way. They can be taken and used in different computers. However, they can be 'write protected' so the data cannot be overwritten. Individual files on a disk can be password protected.

When the data on a disk is no longer required, it can be deleted. Authorisation may need to be given for this in some circumstances.

Data stored on the hard drive of the computer can be deleted. Again, authorisation may be required and the operator must ensure that only appropriate files are deleted.

Staff and Visitor Security Provisions

For many organisations, visitors present a high security risk and must be screened and supervised to varying degrees. Reception staff or security guards may do this, depending on the nature of the business. One of the tools to assist in this area is the use of a reception register, as described on page 54.

Businesses that are most vulnerable include banks, post offices, liquor stores and jewellers. All hold cash or goods of considerable value. Banks are particularly careful to ensure that customers stay on the outside of the counter and only staff and other authorised people are permitted behind the counter. Most of these businesses now have alarms and security devices such as video monitoring and automatic security screens.

Health and safety legislation means that strict visitor security must be implemented in manufacturing plants and other organisations where heavy machinery is used.

Many businesses, particularly those involved in manufacturing, may be at the leading edge of technology in their industries. One of the most valuable assets of these organisations is commercially sensitive information relating to their processing methods. Site visitors provide a very real security threat to the untimely and unauthorised release of this type of information, providing another valid reason to impose stringent visitor security policy.

In some organisations only employees with photo identity cards, pre-programmed number combinations, or computerised cards will have authorised access to the premises. Some Parliamentary offices and military establishments may use such security measures.

Exercise 51

1   Describe what is meant by keeping something:

a   secure

....

....

b   confidential

....

....

2   Describe four procedures that can be carried out to ensure that mail arriving in an office is kept secure and confidential.

a   ....

b   ....

c   ....

d   ....

3   Describe the extra security risk involved when receiving documentation through a fax machine.

....

....

4   What precautions can be taken to prevent unauthorised access to business email?

....

....

....

5   Describe two ways that access to a photocopying machine can be restricted.

a   ....

b   ....

6   Describe the purpose of each of the following.

a   Reception register

....

....

b   Security guards

....

....

Use Business Technology and Equipment

Business equipment and systems provide a raft of tools that can be used to collect, process, organise, output and store information. By becoming familiar with the most common of these options and gaining an understanding of how they work, you can make intelligent decisions about the most efficient and effective technology and equipment to use in a wide variety of situations.

The most obvious place to begin is with the computer. In recent years, computers have become the "hub" of an increasing number of organisations. As well as many tools provided by the computers themselves, they now commonly provide a means of connection and communication for many other types of office equipment and systems.

An Overview of Computer Systems

There are not many offices in Australia today that do not have at least one computer, while most are connected to the Internet and have email facilities.

In a small office stand-alone PCs are often used or linked together with special software which enables sharing of data and a printer.

A more complex network system is used in larger offices in business and government where staff need to communicate with each other and to share work and data, either on the same floor, in the same building or between offices.

Software

Software is available for every type of office requirement. The most commonly used business software is Microsoft Office. Uses for several applications can be found on pages 86 to 90.

In addition to standard office-type programs, the following are examples of specialised software used to manage information in different types of organisations.

Medical Medical software holds patient information and details of medical history, surgery, surgeons' details, appointments, etc.

Dental Dental software includes graphical diagrams where a dentist can enter information about each tooth, either from examination or x-ray. The software can also be used for making appointments. In this way, a history of patients' dental records, appointments, etc is maintained on the computer

Architectural Drawing programs such as CAD (Computer Aided Draughting) are used to produce complex designs for a huge range of construction requirements.

Government Departments Various specialist software is used depending on the department concerned. In many instances software is developed specifically for the purpose required and may be database-oriented.

Computer Set-ups

The Stand-alone PC

The PC (and other hardware and software) is dedicated to one user.

Peer-to-peer Network

A peer-to-peer network (sometimes referred to as a "shared resource system") is a system where independent computers can share "peripherals" such as a laser printer and/or memory and data files.

The main advantage of a peer-to-peer network is the low cost. Windows 9x/2000/XP can be networked by someone with limited networking knowledge, allowing printer sharing, file sharing and other basic network services.

Any computer in a peer-to-peer network can be used as a file server or print server, ie if a printer is hooked up to a computer, that computer becomes the "print server". The components of this type of network simply include the computers that are being used (ie one per person), software (eg Windows 9x/2000/XP), the equipment to be shared (eg printer) and cabling.

A peer-to-peer network is suitable for small businesses using small/medium memory intensive programs and files.

File Server Networks

In this type of network, computers and printers are linked together via a system unit. A network can join users working in the same room or building, different buildings, or different cities. Operators can communicate with each other by using internal electronic mail and can share work or documents.

Novell and Windows are the most common systems used on a file server network. Usually a high-speed, RAM intensive dedicated computer contains the network software and stores users' files/data. Other servers, such as print servers, fax servers or communications servers, may also form part of a network. Each workstation potentially has access to every server on the network; this is dependent on restrictions imposed through the use of passwords. A user has the option of saving files either to their own drive or to the file server and access to files can be restricted as desired.

Often programs (eg Office XP) are stored on each user's hard drive. A network administrator usually looks after large networks. Additional workstations can be added to a file server network at relatively low cost. Components of a file server network include a dedicated file server, Novell or Windows NT software, shared printer(s) and cabling.

File server networks are used by small businesses where file sharing and use of large/many files is required, and by larger businesses located in either the same or several buildings.

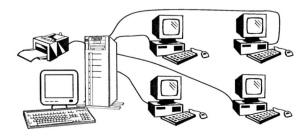

Types of Networks

LAN   Local Area Network – a network in one location, ie a network of computers in one building.

WAN   Wide Area Network – a network that is spread across several sites, eg a company with regional offices may use a WAN to link regional offices.

             The Internet is a WAN spanning the world.

INTRANET   A network within a company with similar services as the Internet, but that can only be used within that organisation (therefore it can hold private, rather than public, information).

The Telephone Communication System

Understand the Phone System

It is necessary for any person who answers incoming calls to have knowledge of the specific telephone system used, and to learn the essential hardware and software components in order to use the system intelligently.

How Many Lines?

Small businesses and sole trader operations might have only one phone line. This means that the line is used for incoming and outgoing phone calls, faxes, and possibly an Internet connection through which email messages are transmitted.

An efficient use of one line is to establish an Internet connection using an ADSL modem. This type of connection uses the telephone line, but allows it to be shared by both voice and data at the same time. This means that an organisation with just one telephone line can be permanently connected to the Internet, and the line will still be available to receive phone calls and faxes.

An awareness of these issues by all staff in an organisation is essential to avoid inefficient use of telephone lines.

Answer Phones

Organisations often use answer phones to assist with incoming calls. These are invaluable for calls received out of normal business hours, where there is a shortage of incoming lines, or to ensure that callers are able to make contact with staff who are unavailable, by leaving a voice message at their telephone extension.

Fax Machines

There are two main types of fax machines: thermal paper fax machines, and plain paper fax machines. Faxes can also be sent from and received by a computer. When a page of information is processed by a fax machine it is digitally converted, or "digitised". The resulting bitmap image is sent via the telephone line to another fax machine, which converts the digital signal back to an analogue image and prints it as a text page.

Fax machines allow businesses to convey written documents or low-resolution images to other businesses and clients immediately, with the information arriving at its destination within a matter of seconds, instead of relying upon the post to deliver the information some time over the following day or two.

The fax machine has been largely superseded over the past few years by email, though there are still instances where a faxed document holds an advantage over email. For example, a pre-printed document needs to be scanned and saved as an image before it can be sent via email attachment, whereas it can be sent immediately (or photocopied and sent, in the case of the page of a book) by fax.

Multi-tasking Abilities

Over the past few years there have been significant developments in fax capability. Even the most basic fax machine is now multi-functional, typically including:

Answer phone

The machine can also be used as a telephone/answer phone system.

Cellular fax

Works in conjunction with a cellular phone. Fax machines may be portable and used in a variety of locations.

Copier

Fax machines can usually be used to copy documents. Some of them have reduction and enlargement capabilities and can print multiple copies.

Electronic telephone directory

Most machines have a fairly large memory to store fax numbers.

Unwanted fax function

Blocks the reception of unwanted faxes.

Automatic redialling

Saves time spent waiting to manually redial when a number is engaged.

Memory dialling

The fax document is scanned and the contents stored in memory. The fax machine then dials the number and transmits the document.

Fax mail out

Multiple fax numbers can be stored in a group; this enables the same document to be sent to the entire group, eliminating the need to individually dial each number.

Microsoft Word has several 'wizards' that can produce custom designed fax forms to serve as cover sheets for outgoing messages. Alternatively, you can produce your own fax cover sheet in Word.

Care Cosmetics
Brisbane Branch

200 Alice Street
Brisbane
Queensland 4000

Fax No: (07) 3452 4392

FACSIMILE

To: *Brian Cooper*

From: *Susan Brown*

Subject: *Gift Baskets*

Fax: *(07) 4334 4521*

Date: *25 September 2002*

No. of pages: *1*
(including cover sheet)

Dear Brian

I confirm our verbal arrangement for 7 x gift baskets at a value of $250 each (including GST) to be delivered to your premises next Monday 30 September.

Activity reports usually print automatically as each fax is sent. This is proof that the fax was transmitted correctly and it can be checked against the telephone bill if necessary.

TRANSACTION REPORT 25-SEP-02 WED 16:15

FOR: CARE COSMETICS - BRISBANE   +61 7 3452 4392

DATE	START	RECEIVER	PAGES	TIME	NOTE
25-SEP	16:14	0743344521	1	1"00"	OK

Transmit Faxes through a Computer System

Faxes can be sent and received through a computer if a modem is used. Modems link a computer to the telephone network. A fax sent to a computer may be viewed on screen, printed and stored.

One of the main disadvantages of this system is that a computer set up to receive faxes must be left on at all times.

Consider the Care Cosmetics scenario at the beginning of the book. Name three ways in which a fax could be used to help manage sales information effectively.

1 ....

....

2 ....

....

3 ....

....

Mobile/Cellular Phones

A mobile phone is simply a radio. The important difference between a cell phone and a conventional radio, aside from the frequency range they operate within, is that a mobile phone can both transmit and receive, making it a two-way radio. Depending on the type of phone, the radio waves transmitted and received can be either digital or analogue.

The cell phone has revolutionised business by providing instant communication between company and clients, as well as between company and staff. Continual contact can be maintained between a company and its representatives while they are away from the premises, and fresh information can be conveyed immediately between the two parties. Clients and potential clients of small businesses can also contact sole business operators while they are away from their base, and in many cases mobile phones have eliminated the need for smaller businesses to operate an office at all.

An advantage of mobile phones is their flexibility, especially for people who are on the move. This includes bank personnel, land agents and sales representatives.

In addition to the advantages associated with the mobility of cell phones, they also provide an extension of an organisation's telephone communication system. Mobile phones can act as answering services, receive faxes, send and receive text and email messages, and access the Internet – all without using the traditional telephone landlines. This degree of functionality means that cell phones are becoming increasingly important as a communication tool for organisations.

Pager

A pager is a communications device that allows people who are unable to answer a phone to take short messages. It is, like the mobile phone, a radio device, though most pagers in current use are one-way devices that only *receive* signals.

Until quite recently the main purpose of pagers was to alert the user to the fact that someone was trying to contact them, usually beeping, then flashing a short message containing abbreviated details. New generations of pagers offer two-way paging, and even contain a small virtual keyboard on the tiny LCD screen that allows users to type messages in return. They can also deliver pre-programmed replies, such as "Yes", "No", or "I'll be late". Today's pagers include the ability to send and receive brief email messages. Internal memory allows the user to store a number of saved messages, while some pagers come with a data cable for connection to a PC, to facilitate the download of addresses and phone numbers from the user's email address book.

1   What has traditionally been the main use of a pager?

    ....

    ....

2   Explain in your own words the main advantages for business people in using a mobile phone.

    ....

    ....

    ....

    ....

3   When would a fax machine be more advantageous than using email?

    ....

    ....

The Telephone Network in Computing

Telephone Networks

WANs often make use of public networks such as the public telephone system. Before we look at telephone networks it is important to understand how data is transmitted along a telephone line.

Digital and Analogue

A computer is a *digital* device and carries out most of its functions by turning on or off a series of electronic switches, ie it is <u>non-continuous</u>.   A binary 0, which is shown below as a circle, represents a switch that is turned off; a binary 1, which is shown as a square, indicates that the switch is on. The following is a representation of digital code.

A telephone system is an *analogue* device which is designed to transmit the various sounds and tones of the human voice.   These sounds are sent electronically in an analogue signal as a <u>continuous</u> electronic current, which can be represented as a wavy line shown below.

Modems

A *modem* is used to convert digital data into analogue signals so it can be sent through the telephone system. At the receiving end a modem converts the analogue signals back into digital code.

modem card

Internet

The Internet is an international network of millions of computers that allows you to access and transmit information. The Internet can be accessed by anyone who has a computer, modem with phone line, browser software and access to an Internet service provider's Internet link.

The following diagram represents how PCs interact with the Internet.

- Personal Computers (PCs) can only gain access to the Internet via an **Internet Service Provider (ISP)**.

- The ISP is connected to the Internet and provides Internet access to end users.

- Every ISP on the Internet is connected to one or more ISPs.

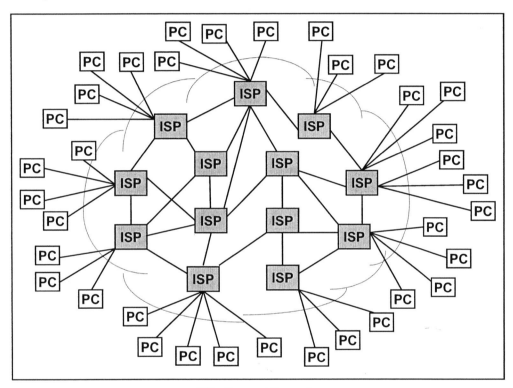

PC = Personal Computer
ISP = Internet Service Provider

A PC displayed in the diagram above could also be called a *client*. A client is a personal computer or workstation that is connected to a server. In the diagram above, the clients are connected to their respective ISP's servers.

An ISP displayed in the diagram above uses a *server* to manage its network resources. A server manages files, folders, web sites, network communications, and accounts, allowing access to the Internet. It allows clients to access data from one common location.

Intranet

An Intranet is a local Internet. It works in a similar way to the Internet but can only be accessed from within a company's network. It cannot be accessed outside the company's system. The web pages displayed within an Intranet usually have a similar appearance to those on the Internet but are generally not as graphical and flashy – pages are required to display quickly to ensure staff can locate information efficiently.

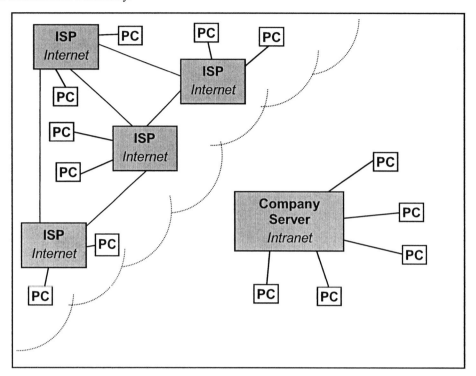

An Intranet allows a company to disseminate information quickly and easily to its staff. Reference material relating to any product can be kept on the Intranet so any staff member can instantly refer to the material instead of looking up the data in a manual, which may be outdated. A normal web browser is used to display data from an Intranet.

Resources for staff can also be found on an Intranet – templates, spreadsheets, databases, presentations, etc. to which information may be added or used as required. Access may also be provided to software utilities and plug-ins required for different applications.

Extranet

An Extranet is an Intranet that can be accessed from the Internet. A company executive can log on to the Internet and go to a web site address. A user name and password is required to gain access to the company's data.

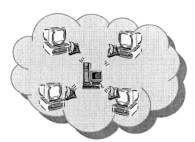

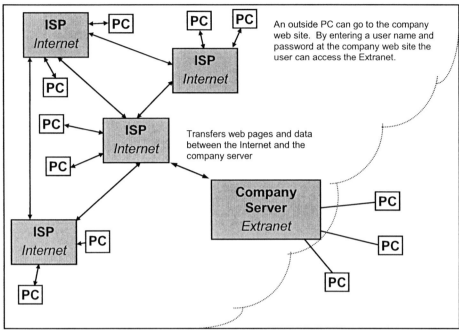

An Extranet allows a company to disseminate information quickly and easily to its staff outside the company network. Staff members can log in at the company's web site using a web browser and can access email, view reference material, access files, templates, databases, etc.

Customers can also be allocated an account number and password to access their account, view and order items etc. A customer can view products and specials online without having to wait for brochures or a sales representative to call them. In some cases when a customer orders a product they can track its progress through the system and see whether their order has been completed and sent. They can also enquire about certain products by sending an email message.

Exercise 54

The difference between an *Intranet* and an *Extranet* is:

....

....

....

....

Email

In Section 1, we discussed how email is used to communicate and to collect information. Its usage extends to all areas of managing information – it can be used to efficiently gather, collate, disseminate and store information.

The advantages of using email are many.

- It's fast;
- It's cheap;
- It's convenient; (You don't even have to go to the Post Office!)
- Files can be attached and sent with your message; (There is no need to copy files onto a disk and send through the post.)
- Businesses can easily communicate between branch offices within the same country, or from country to country.

To be able to use email you need:

- An account with an Internet Service Provider
- A computer and modem with telephone line
- Web browser software which contains an email program

When you have chosen your Internet Service Provider you will be given information about your account and how to connect to their system together with a CD to set up your email configuration. Some of the information you may be given is shown below.

Username and password	The account name and password will be used when logging onto the Internet Service Provider's system. The same account name and password is usually used to access your email.
Domain name	The name of your company, eg softwarepublications.com.au, or Internet Service Provider, eg ozemail.com.au
Email address	The address that people can use to send email messages to you. This is usually your name then the domain name, eg catherineperkins@softwarepublications.com.au
DNS server	A Domain Name Server converts domain names into IP addresses.
IP address	The Internet protocol (IP) address is a unique address used by you to connect to the Internet.

In a company environment where a LAN is used the email software will be configured by a technician or network administrator. It is likely that the company will have its own domain name – each employee generally uses their own name and the company's domain name for their email address, eg ray.brown@denstore.com.au; ann.smith@denstore.com.au.

Other Business Equipment

Photocopier

A photocopier copies an image onto another sheet of paper or plastic film.

The photocopier is a key piece of equipment in managing information effectively. Multiple copies of information can be made quickly and easily, allowing several people to have a copy of one document.

Printer

A printer is a peripheral device that connects to a computer, allowing the computer user to reproduce on paper what is displayed on screen. Printers vary in speed, size, sophistication and cost, depending upon the purposes for which they are required.

They fall into two main categories: impact and non-impact. Impact printers include dot matrix and daisy wheel printers, while non-impact printers cover a much larger range, including laser and ink-jet printers. Impact printers are generally noisier than non-impact printers.

Impact printers are usually used for a specific purpose in an organisation. For example, they are frequently used to print invoices, because they are able to produce carbon copies, providing hard copy invoice duplicates.

Impact printers still provide the cheapest method of printing plain text, so while the quality of output isn't high, they are frequently suitable for internal reports that are printed often and may be quite large, eg a daily trial balance.

Ink-jet printers are the cheapest type of printer to purchase. However, running costs over the long term are considerably greater than for the initially more expensive laser printer. Ink-jet printers can produce high quality colour output, but tend to be slower than laser printers.

Laser printers are very much like photocopiers in construction and operation, and because of the high cost of colour models, most lasers in standard use only print in black.

Printers enable organisations to produce in-house documents, transparencies, brochures and pamphlets, newsletters and technical manuals without having to contract a specialist company to do the job.

Multimedia Projector

A projector uses a lens and a light source to transfer an image onto a blank wall or a projection screen.

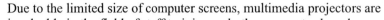

Although the earliest multimedia projectors worked only with film, transparencies and slides, most projectors today are digital or a combination of digital and analogue, and are capable of transmitting information from a computer monitor. This makes them an ideal tool to use for presenting information to a group.

Due to the limited size of computer screens, multimedia projectors are invaluable in the field of staff training and other computer-based presentations. Large audiences

can view projected information along with sound, without the expense of multiple individual computer monitors.

Products and services can be demonstrated to potential clients and other interested parties by using a projector in, for example, a sales meeting or at a trade show.

Exercise 55

1   Explain the difference in function between a photocopier and a printer.

    ....

    ....

    ....

2   Give two examples of items that you would photocopy in an office and two examples of items you would print.

    Photocopy:

    a   ....

    b   ....

    Print:

    a   ....

    b   ....

3   When buying a new printer, list three considerations that you would take into account.

    a   ....

    b   ....

    c   ....

4   Give three examples of situations when a multimedia projector would be useful.

    a   ....

    b   ....

    c   ....

Laptop Computer

A laptop computer (otherwise known as a notebook), is a computer that contains its own battery power source and is completely portable because it is a convenient size, the hard drive and screen are linked, and it does not need to be plugged in. Laptops can also run off AC (mains) power. Special docking stations allow a laptop computer to connect to a conventional desktop monitor, keyboard and printer for ease of use at the company base.

Due to their portability, laptop computers can be used to collect, organise, present and disseminate information "on the spot". Meeting attendees can take electronic notes while at meetings and seminars; sales and marketing staff are able to create and display slideshows of company products and/or services to clients while they are away from base.

Exercise 56

1   Give two advantages and two disadvantages of a laptop.

Advantages:

a ....

b ....

Disadvantages:

a ....

b ....

2   Explain briefly what problems organisations would have faced before the invention of photocopiers.

....

....

....

....

....

Personal Digital Assistant

Palmtop computers and Personal Digital Assistants (PDAs) are very small handheld computers that can fit in the palm of the hand and be carried in a coat pocket. They are completely portable, contain their own power source, and present a low-cost alternative to a laptop computer when all the extra features of a laptop are not required.

Palmtop/PDA computers use a different operating system (usually Windows CE) to laptop and desktop computers, with all programs preinstalled into the computer's ROM – no installation of programs is required. Because of this, they can be switched on and off instantly with no waiting time for the operating system or programs to load.

Organise Information in a Useful Format

There are many ways in which information can be organised, depending on its final use. Among the most flexible and useful tools is the huge range of computer applications available to collect, sort, calculate, output and present information.

Windows

In most instances "Windows" application programs such as Microsoft Word, Excel, PageMaker, etc are used with Windows 9x/2000/XP.

Windows application programs have the following advantages.

- They have the same "look" and "feel" about them, enabling users to easily learn different programs.

- Windows has a *graphical user interface* (GUI) which means that what you see on your page is what you get when a file is printed (or close to it!). For example, fonts, columns, graphics, etc will be printed as they appear on screen.

- You can "multi-task", ie use more than one file and/or program at a time.

- Data from one program can be moved/copied into another program.

The following picture shows how your screen might look if you had several programs in Microsoft Office XP running at the same time.

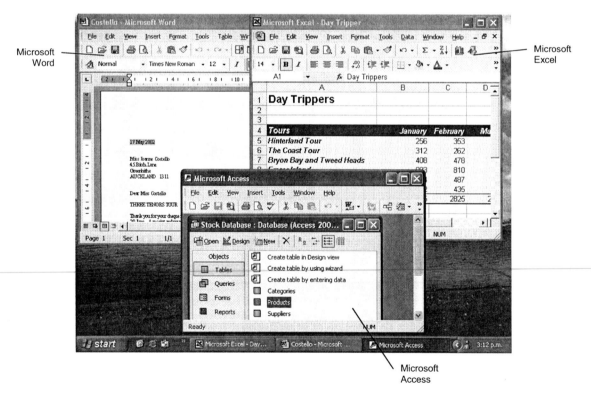

© Software Educational Resources Ltd

Word Processing Software

A word processing program allows you to create text and/or graphics using a keyboard and screen. Data is stored on disk so it can be recalled to the screen and edited and reformatted as many times as required. One or more copies of a file can be printed during this process.

Some programs such as Microsoft Word have desktop publishing and calculation capabilities.

Tasks carried out with a word processing program include the creation of:

- Letters and other general correspondence, eg memos, faxes

- Minutes of meetings, financial documents, reports, travel documents

- Flyers, advertisements

- Tables, mail merges, labels

- Brochures, manuals

Touring Guides

	US $	CAN $	AUS $	NZ $
AA Bed and Breakfast/Britain	13.95	16.95	18.95	32.95
AA Big Road Atlas/Britain	9.95	12.95	14.95	27.95
AA Tour Guide: Scotland	14.95	18.95	19.95	35.95
AA Tour Guide: Britain	16.95	19.95	22.95	39.95
AA Scottish Highlands	18.95	22.95	24.95	39.95
Insight Guide: Scotland	19.95	19.95	24.95	43.95
Insight Guide: Britain	12.95	16.95	14.95	27.95
Insight Enjoy Scotland	8.95	9.95	10.95	17.95
Scotland Bed and Breakfast	12.95	12.95	14.95	23.95
Scotland Hotels/ Guest Houses	8.95	8.95	9.95	14.95
Scotland More than 1001 Things	9.95	10.95	12.95	19.95
Scotland Touring Map	7.95	6.95	7.95	11.95

Spreadsheet Software

A spreadsheet is essentially a large chart composed entirely of rectangular pigeon holes (called cells). A spreadsheet is made up of rows and columns. The data that is entered into cells can be stored as values, text, numbers or formulas. When figures are updated the entire spreadsheet will reflect the changes made because formulas contain "cell references" rather than actual figures. The data entered can then be saved as a file and opened at a later date.

Charts can be created in a variety of different styles to show the data in visual form. When the spreadsheet data is changed, the information in the chart is updated.

Spreadsheets are widely used:

In industry and commerce

For financial accounts; forecasting and projecting results; recording and comparing data; personnel details.

At home

For budgeting (eg savings and travelling expenses); calculations (eg painting, wallpapering).

By schools

For test and examination results; timetables; school rolls.

By clubs

For membership fees; sports results; sponsorship details.

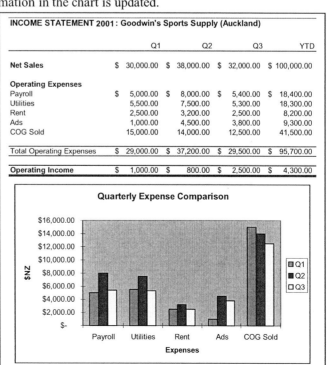

INCOME STATEMENT 2001 : Goodwin's Sports Supply (Auckland)

	Q1	Q2	Q3	YTD
Net Sales	$ 30,000.00	$ 38,000.00	$ 32,000.00	$ 100,000.00
Operating Expenses				
Payroll	$ 5,000.00	$ 8,000.00	$ 5,400.00	$ 18,400.00
Utilities	5,500.00	7,500.00	5,300.00	18,300.00
Rent	2,500.00	3,200.00	2,500.00	8,200.00
Ads	1,000.00	4,500.00	3,800.00	9,300.00
COG Sold	15,000.00	14,000.00	12,500.00	41,500.00
Total Operating Expenses	$ 29,000.00	$ 37,200.00	$ 29,500.00	$ 95,700.00
Operating Income	$ 1,000.00	$ 800.00	$ 2,500.00	$ 4,300.00

Database Software

Database software is used to manage, sort and manipulate data. It can be used to keep track of stock, client details, staff details, etc. You can input data using a form or table.

Data can be extracted using queries (questions) to display specific data.

Reports can be generated to give a copy (which is usually printed) of all the data in the database or an in-depth look at particular information only. A report can be based on a query to show data relating to a specified question only. Labels and graphs can also be produced.

Uses for a database include:

- Keeping records of club membership
- Client records for companies
- Student records and results
- Stock control
- Medical information, eg patient details
- Events
- Reference, eg libraries, videos
- Staff records
- Asset records

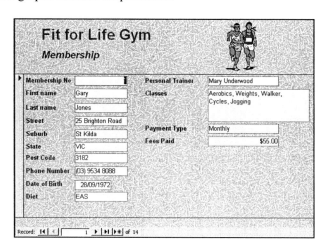

Desktop Publishing Software

Desktop publishing is the production of high visual impact documents, magazines, newspaper pages, etc. Various types of graphics can be printed on the same page including lines, boxes, shapes, photographs and illustrations.

The printed output can be distributed as it is, photocopied or used as camera-ready copy for an offset printer.

The concept of producing a document using desktop publishing software is entirely different to producing a document using a word processing program. Desktop publishing techniques require the layout of a page to be planned in advance, to allocate areas for pictures, graphic displays, etc.

Text and/or graphics can be imported from other programs.

Examples of desktop publishing programs currently used are Adobe PageMaker, Microsoft Publisher and Quark XPress.

Desktop publishing software is mostly used to create:

- Flyers, advertisements, brochures
- Invitations, business cards, business stationery, eg letterheads, faxes
- Books
- Newsletters
- Advertising copy

Graphics and Presentation Software

Different types of graphics and presentation software are available, each with their own special capabilities. Macromedia FreeHand is used to edit and enhance graphics (pictures) which can then be used in desktop publishing (and word processing) programs. Adobe PhotoShop provides similar functionality for use with photographs.

Presentation programs such as PowerPoint enable you to create a slide show with graphics and sound enhancements, for example you could promote a product to an audience using a computer and data projector. Slides, handouts and overhead transparencies can be created using a presentation program.

Communications Software

The benefits of using the Internet and email to manage information have been well covered in this book already. The software needed to utilise these tools is user-friendly, and usually free!

Web Browser Software

A Web Browser is a software program that allows you to view information on the Internet. The two most commonly used are Microsoft Internet Explorer and Netscape Navigator. Microsoft Internet Explorer is included with some Microsoft products. Web Browsers are usually available through your Internet Service Provider or can be downloaded from the Internet. Most providers will give you a free CD (or disks) with a setup program that will load the Web Browser and set up your Internet connection.

Email Software

Email software allows you to send and receive messages across the Internet. There are many different email programs available. Microsoft Internet Explorer 6.0 includes Outlook Express which is similar to the email facility in Outlook 2002 (used in Section 1) in Office XP.

Accounting Software

Accounting software allows the financial records of an organisation to be computerised. Tasks such as invoicing, ordering items, making and receiving payments, updating ledger accounts, preparing bank deposits and reconciling accounts are all completed in the accounting package. Financial reports used to run an organisation, such as trial balances and profit and loss reports, may be printed up-to-date at any time. Accounting packages may also include payroll/wages processing.

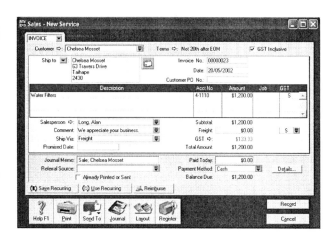

Computer Aided Design Software

The design of anything from common household items right through to cars, boats and houses is done using computers these days. CAD (Computer Aided Design) software applications are used by engineers, architects, artists, draughters and many others to create technical illustrations and precision drawings. CAD is often associated with CAM (Computer Aided Manufacturing), which carries the concept of computer aided design through into the manufacturing process.

Most modern items in your home will have been designed by computer. So too will your car, your boat, caravan, jet-ski and your sporting equipment, your home, garage, garden shed and glasshouse. The accuracy and precision obtained by using computer aided design gives manufacturers the ability to create a near-perfect product, exactly the same every time, with exact proportions and critical measurements. This reduces the chances of recall or the return for credit of inferior products, and considerably less man-hours are used in both the development and manufacture of those products.

Exercise 57

Identify the most appropriate type of application to use to create:

A company logo ....

A customer details list ....

A budget ....

Multimedia Software

Multimedia software can be broken down into various areas: sound, graphics, animation and video. Because of the widespread use of the Internet, the use of multimedia software has increased. Programs such as RealOne Player, QuickTime, Yahoo! Player and many more are used to play sounds, animations and video either from the Internet or from your PC.

Multimedia software can be used to produce:

- Insurance plans and house designs that can be presented to clients via multimedia applications on laptop computers.

- Vinyl and other signs that can be applied to vehicles and buildings.

- Interactive training using computers.

- Movie animation.

- Websites.

- On-line surveys.

Exercise 58

Choose two of the following software applications and write a brief description of each, mentioning one example of what could be created in that program.

Word Processing * Desktop Publishing * Computer-Aided Design * Communications

1   ....

     ....

2   ....

     ....

Create a Spreadsheet

In Section 1 the scenario of buying mobile phones for Care Cosmetics staff within budgetary confinements was considered, and a working plan for a spreadsheet to solve the problem was prepared.

The spreadsheet developed from the working plan is illustrated below.

	A	B	C	D	E	F	G
1	**Care Cosmetics Staff**						
2	**Mobile Phone Packages**						
3							
4			**Mobile Phone Model**	**Phone Cost**	**Monthly Cost**	**Extra Costs**	**Initial Cost**
5	*Claire*	Package 1	Nokia 5510	599	120	160	879
6		Package 2	Siemens ME45	869	100	100	1069
7	*Richard*	Package 1	Alcatel 511	379	80	50	509
8		Package 2	Nokia 3315	349	120	70	539
9	*Brent*	Package 1	Alcatel 311	219	15	0	234
10		Package 2	Ericsson A3618	199	20	0	219
11							

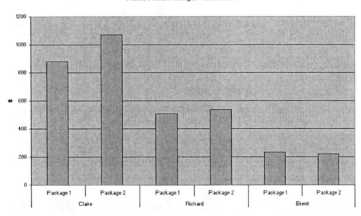

Mobile Phone Packages - Initial Cost

Exercise 59

In Exercise 5 you created a working plan as part of the process of developing usable sales information for Care Cosmetics. Compare your working plan with the plan on the next page. Are there significant differences between the two? If so, will both options still solve the problem, or do some adjustments need to be made to your working plan?

Spreadsheet Working Plan

Purpose

The purpose of the spreadsheet is to collect and present monthly sales results for Care Cosmetics, by branch, and to display comparisons between branches and from month to month.

Spreadsheet features to be used

AutoSum, Chart, Borders, fonts, Average.

Spreadsheet Specifications

November Sales											
	Week 1	Week 2	Week 3	Week 4	Average						
Sydney				➤	=AVERAGE( )						
Melbourne				➤	=AVERAGE( )						
Brisbane				➤	=AVERAGE( )						
Perth				➤	=AVERAGE( )						
Total	$	$	$	$	=AVERAGE( )						

File name and Location of Spreadsheet

C:\My Documents\Care Cosmetics - November

Exercise 60

The spreadsheet in this exercise is based on the working plan on the previous page.

1   Launch Excel from the All Programs menu on the Start button, or from the icon on your
    Windows Desktop.

2   In a new workbook create the worksheet displayed below.

	A	B	C	D	E
1	Care Cosmetics				
2	November Sales				
3					
4		Week 1	Week 2	Week 3	Week 4
5					
6	Sydney	5612	4587	5874	6012
7	Melbourne	6566	5644	5987	5740
8	Brisbane	4422	3754	4671	4007
9	Perth	2886	2950	3520	3610
10					
11	Total				

3   Click in cell A1, apply bold formatting and increase the font size to 14.

4   Change the formatting of cell A2 to bold and 12 pt font size.

5   Select cells B4 to E4, then apply bold, italics and right alignment.

6   Click on the ▾ of the Borders button ⊞ ▾ and choose the Bottom
    Border option.

7   Format cells B6 to E9 as Numbers with no decimal places and a
    thousands separator.

8   Apply bold formatting to cell A11.

9   Select cells B11 to E11 and click on the AutoSum button ∑ to total the sales figures for
    each week.

10 Format cells B11 to E11 as Currency with no decimal places.

11 Add a Top and Thick Bottom border to cells A11 to E11.

12 Save the workbook as **Care Cosmetics Sales**

Create an Average Formula

Exercise 61

1   Click in cell F4 and type: **Average Sales**

    Press Ctrl Enter to confirm the contents and remain in the same cell.

2   Click on cell E4 then click on the Format Painter button.

3   Click on cell F4 to copy the format from cell E4.

4   To widen column F, choose [Format] Column, AutoFit Selection.

5 Click in cell F6. Click on the AutoSum button . Select Average from the list and press Ctrl Enter.

6 Click on the Fill Handle as shown and drag down cells F7 to F11. The calculation will be copied and modified for each cell.

5,521

Fill Handle

7 Delete the calculation in cell F10.

8 Use the Format Painter button to copy the format from cell E11 to cell F11.

9 Save the changes to the workbook.

Create a Bar Chart

Exercise 62

1 Select cells A4 to E9.

2 Press F11 on the keyboard. A bar chart will be created in a new worksheet.

3 Choose [Chart] Chart Options.

4 In the Chart title: box of the Titles tab type: **Care Cosmetics – November Sales**

5 Add the Category (X) axis: and Value (Y) axis: headings as shown below.

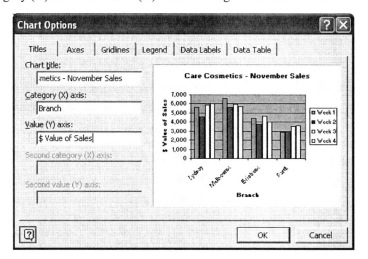

6 Click on OK to add the headings to the chart.

7 Double click on the Chart1 sheet tab and type: **November Sales Chart**

8 Press Enter to confirm the new name of the worksheet, then save the changes.

Create a Pie Chart

Exercise 63

1 Click on the Sheet1 tab.

2 Rename the worksheet: **November Sales**

3 Select cells A6 to A9, then hold Ctrl and select cells F6 to F9.

4 Click on the Chart Wizard button and select ● Pie from the Chart type: list.

5 Click on the Pie with a 3-D visual effect option in the Chart sub-type: section.

6 Click on Next >, then on Next > again.

7   In the Chart title: box type: **Average Sales for November**

8   In the Legend tab, click in the *Bottom* option in the Placement section, to place the legend beneath the chart.

9   Click on the Data Labels tab and click in the *Value* option in the Label Contains section.

10   Click on ⬚ Next > and ensure the *As object in:* option is chosen to place the pie chart in the November Sales worksheet.

11   Click on ⬚ Finish to display the chart.

12   Click and drag the chart it to reposition it as displayed below.

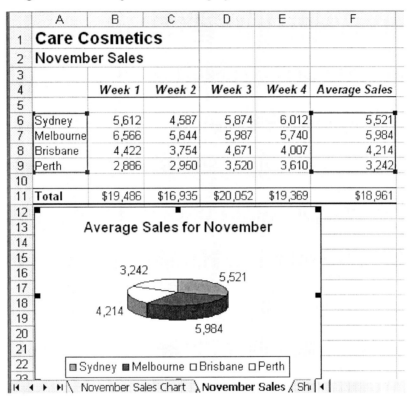

13   Using the handle at the lower right corner, resize the chart so that it covers cells A12 to F27.

14   Double click on the title Average Sales for November and click on the Font tab in the Format Chart Title dialog box. Change the font size to 10 pt. Click on OK.

15   Double click on the Data Labels (on the Pie Chart), change the font to 8 pt and click on OK.

16   Save the changes to the workbook.

Spreadsheet Documentation

If you are creating spreadsheets for other people to use, or spreadsheets that are complex and are used infrequently, documentation provides essential assistance to users.

Clear documentation can give an understanding of the use and purpose of a spreadsheet together with instructions on how to use and manipulate it. Documentation can be inserted into a spreadsheet in a blank area or as separate worksheet, eg a worksheet named Documentation. Alternatively, documentation may be created in Word.

The following guidelines summarise how to create clear documentation.

Title

Ensure your documentation has a title. Include a subtitle with the date the spreadsheet was completed and the author. You may wish to include the company name, department and any other relevant details.

Purpose

Write a paragraph explaining the purpose of the spreadsheet. Include the final outcome that will be achieved by using the spreadsheet.

Installation Instructions

If the spreadsheet is a template you will need to indicate this, and how to use it.

General Instructions

A simple outline of the structure of the spreadsheet should be given to provide the user with an overall picture. Include instructions on how to use the spreadsheet, what data is to be inserted where, which data can be altered, printing the spreadsheet, viewing charts, etc. Mention if there are any links in the spreadsheet, to another file or within the spreadsheet, and their purpose. It is advantageous to use named ranges when creating a spreadsheet as these may be used instead of cell references to provide clarity to your documentation.

Remember, the purpose of documentation is to help the user to understand your spreadsheet, not to teach them how to use the spreadsheet program.

Not all spreadsheets in the average office would be documented extensively unless multiple users required such instructions.

Basic spreadsheet documentation can be inserted at the top of a worksheet but if it is more complex it is tidier to include it on the first worksheet of a workbook.

The following worksheet shows documentation for the Care Cosmetics Mobile Phones scenario (pages 5 and 6).

	A	B	C	D	E
1	**Mobile Phone Packages**				
2	*Julia Donaldson - 12 October 2002*				
3					
4	**Purpose**				
5	Identify which mobile phone packages suggested by staff members are within budget.				
6					
7					
8	**Installation**				
9	Copy file to the My Documents folder.				
10					
11					
12	**General Instructions**				
13	To add an additional package - insert a blank row and enter data.				
14	To add a new staff member - insert new rows under existing staff members' details.				
15	Use the AutoSum button when calculating the Initial Cost.				
16					
17					
18	**Macros**				
19	**Name**	**Purpose**	**Shortcut Key**	**Menu Option**	**Other Details**
20	PrintData	Prints worksheet data only	Ctrl Shift Y		
21	PrintChart	Prints chart only	Ctrl Shift H		
22					
23					

Initial cost chart / Phone cost info \ **Documentation** / Sheet3 /

Exercise 64

In a separate worksheet in the Care Cosmetics Sales workbook, complete documentation for the spreadsheet created in exercises 60 to 63. Explain how the workbook can be saved with another name and used to record the sales for each new month. Save and close the workbook, and close Excel.

How could the Care Cosmetics Sales workbook be used more efficiently than saving a copy of the previous month's file?

....

....

Communicate Information

Learning Outcomes

At the end of this section you should be able to -

❑   Communicate information to relevant people in an organisation.

❑   Identify and solve difficulties in accessing and organising information.

Communicate Information Effectively

Presenting information in a way that is interesting, understandable and relevant, is an integral part of how useful the information is perceived to be. A boring, uninformative presentation, even with the most relevant and accurate information, will probably result in the information being misused, underutilised, or completely forgotten about.

Communication Tips

Choose your time carefully

It is important to let others know how much of their time will be required. As well as being courteous, this reduces the chance of your audience becoming distracted by other tasks, or trying to hurry you along.

Example

"I'd like to explain the new sales results collection procedures to you. Could I have half an hour of your time over the next few days?"

"Sure, I'll be free on Wednesday afternoon, give me a call then."

"Good. Shall we say 2.00 pm?"

Decide what information to give

1   Establish what information is required. Give the key information required first.

2   Offer to discuss or explain further if required.

3   Provide brochures, handouts, examples or other supporting material where applicable.

4   If you are asked a question to which you do not know the answer, undertake to find the correct answer.

Present information in an interesting format

1   Greet your audience, smile and introduce yourself if you are not already known to them.

2   State your topic right at the beginning, and if possible write it on a whiteboard or display it on an overhead projector.

3   Tell the audience whether or not you invite questions during the presentation or if you would prefer them to wait until the end.

4   If you are delivering a lecture-type presentation, and have handouts, tell your audience that you will be handing out notes at the end. Some speakers prefer to hand out notes at the beginning so that the audience can follow along with the presentation, while others prefer to hand them out at the end so that they have the audience's full attention during the presentation.

5   Do not use technical terms when addressing a group who may not have any idea what you are talking about. Know your audience!

Be yourself

You do not need to take on another persona when you stand up and speak to a group of people. However, it is vital that you do tailor your language to suit the group. It is never appropriate to use "colourful" language when speaking to a group – it is likely to distract from what you are saying, and may easily be found offensive by others.

Use a computer application

If you are a competent PowerPoint user, it can make a presentation more interesting. However, do not try to dazzle the audience with your incredible PowerPoint skills, by animating each slide and incorporating every special effect in the program. A presentation that is too "busy" will detract from the message you are delivering and could annoy the audience rather than amaze them.

Keep listeners' attention

1   If you are speaking to a group, try directing your attention to various people in the room, one at a time. Make eye contact and speak directly to that person for a minute or so.

2   Ask questions. Whether they are rhetorical or demand some kind of response, questions keep the listener involved. When it comes to communicating, a two-way conversation is usually more effective than a lecture.

To finish

Find a way to check that your main points have been understood. Ask questions of your audience, invite them to question you, and/or involve everyone in a quick workshop or exercise during the meeting.

Plan a Presentation

The next few pages will assist in planning a presentation, from a talk, to a large scale product demonstration, whether it is to a small group or an auditorium full of people. The more planning and thought that is put into a presentation, the easier it is to present.

There are six main steps to producing a presentation.

Step 1

- Decide on the topic.

  - Select the presentation method to be used.
  - Will you use overhead transparencies or slides?
  - Will a projector be used for your presentation?
  - Are you going to provide handouts?

- Decide on a location.

  - Check the location is available, is of an appropriate size and convenient for the audience to get to.
  - Check the room temperature is correct (you do not want your audience falling asleep because the room is too hot).
  - Check there is enough lighting and know where the lights can be turned on/off and dimmed as required.
  - If it is a large room check that a microphone can be used and that it can be tested before your presentation.

- Know the date, start time and length of the presentation.

- Understand the type of audience who will be attending your presentation. Any of the following may be relevant:

  - Knowledge
  - Interests
  - Point of view (are they likely to be agreeing with you or to need persuading?)
  - Male/female ratio
  - Age
  - Approximate number that will be attending.

- What will the presentation cost? Items to consider are:

  - Room hire plus chairs, refreshments provided, etc.
  - Rental of any equipment, eg data projector, laptop.
  - Cost of materials and services used to create the presentation, eg cost of overhead transparencies, slides.
  - Cost of audience materials, eg name tags, notes, hand-outs, brochures.

Step 2

- Gather information on the content of your presentation.

  □ Organise the content into a logical order. The order of a presentation should be: introduction, body of the presentation and a conclusion.

  □ Decide on the information that will appear on slides/handout pages/overhead transparencies.

  □ Ensure the length of the presentation will fit within the time frame allocated.

Step 3

- Set up the content of the presentation.

  □ Test drive a couple of slides on the equipment (overhead transparencies, slide projector or OHT/data projector) to ensure that any fonts, colours, objects, pictures, etc display as required.

  □ Complete the presentation based on the content collected in Step 2 and using the information gained from the test drive.

  □ Ensure that the order of the presentation flows well. Topics should be presented in a logical order that the audience can understand.

Step 4

- Rehearse the presentation by yourself. Run through it at least twice before presenting to another person.

  □ If using a projector rehearse the presentation on screen at the computer.

  □ If you are demonstrating or using other equipment in your presentation, be sure to include these in your rehearsal.

  □ Try out your presentation in front of another person. Their feedback can help polish a presentation.

Step 5

- Arrive early for your presentation.

  □ Set up and test any equipment required to ensure that everything is working correctly, ahead of time.

  □ Make sure that all lights are on at the start of the presentation. This will help your audience find a seat. Once the audience is settled you will be able to introduce yourself and the topic. The lights can then be dimmed. Remember not to dim the lights too much as the audience will want to see you and they might want to take notes.

Step 6

- Once the presentation is over, evaluate the effectiveness of it. Was the content valid? Was there enough time to finish the presentation? Were you able to communicate with the audience comfortably? Did all the equipment work?

Action Plan - Summary

Step 1

- Decide on a topic and select the presentation method
- Decide on a location and know the date, start time and length of the presentation
- Understand the type of audience who will be attending your presentation
- Determine the cost of the presentation/equipment

Step 2

- Gather the information
- Organise the information in a logical order
- How will the information appear?
- Ensure the presentation fits within the time frame

Step 3

- Set up the content in PowerPoint
- Test drive the presentation on the equipment
- Complete the presentation, modifying anything found to be problematic in the test drive
- Ensure the order flows well

Step 4

- Rehearse the presentation alone twice
- Rehearse using the projector and any equipment demonstration
- Rehearse with another person for their feedback

Step 5

- Arrive early at the presentation
- Set up and test equipment and check lighting
- Deliver the presentation

Step 6

- Evaluate the presentation afterwards

Exercise 65

Imagine you are going to present sales results to the Care Cosmetics Board of Directors at their next meeting. The following list contains the tasks you need to complete to begin planning your presentation. Change the list to reflect the order in which the tasks must be completed, by numbering the list (1 to 11), or reproducing it in a Word document.

.... Set up the content of the presentation.

.... Check the room where the presentation will take place.

.... Rehearse the presentation.

.... Evaluate how the presentation went.

.... Work out the cost of the presentation.

.... Sort the presentation into a logical order.

.... Gather information for the presentation.

.... Decide on the type of presentation.

.... Decide on a venue for the presentation.

.... Decide on the date and length of the presentation.

.... Identify the target audience.

Use PowerPoint to Present Information

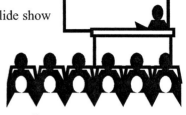

Presentation programs such as PowerPoint enable you to create a slide show with graphics and sound enhancements.

PowerPoint 2002 is a software program designed to help present information to an audience of any size. The information presented could be in the form of handouts, overhead transparencies, slides or on-screen slides using a data projector. Whichever form is utilised the information must be clear, concise and appropriate to your audience.

Presentation Elements

Elements of a presentation that you might want to take into consideration when creating and delivering a presentation are listed below. Not all elements will suit all presentations; they are given only as a guide.

Content

- Research your content well from reliable sources.

- If you are having difficulty establishing enough content, jot keywords relating to your topic on a piece of paper, whether they are positive or negative. The keywords may help you to define areas of interest that you can use in your presentation.

- Think about the audience and the questions they may have for you regarding the topic – some of these could be answered in your presentation.

- Talk to people who are involved with the topic you are presenting.

- Think about the demographics of your audience – sex, age, ability, knowledge, interest, expectations, etc. Ensure that the presentation will meet their requirements.

- How many people will be attending? Should the presentation be formal or informal? Typically, larger groups constitute a more formal presentation whereas for smaller groups the presentation can be less formal.

- Categorise your notes. This assists in placing presentation topics in a logical order.

- Analyse whether your presentation will build up to a climax or final goal – if so ensure each step in the presentation is clearly defined in a logical order building up to the final goal.

- Add examples so the audience can understand a problem and see the solution. Real life examples provide a great method of getting a message across.

- Add contrast to a topic – for and against; positive and negative.

- Add comparisons of "this" against "that".

- Remember to check copyright issues when adding content from various sources. Do you need permission to use the material?

Text

- When using typed text select a sans serif font and large size for clarity. 30 pt or above will make the text in a presentation easier for the audience to read.

- Use different fonts sparingly; too many can make a slide/handout hard to read.

- Try not to use italics as they can be hard to read from a projected screen.

- Stay away from script fonts like Brush Script, Freestyle Script, etc as these are hard to read.

- Use different font sizes to indicate the level of headings in a slide. A major heading should appear in the largest font size, subheadings in a smaller size and the body of text in a font size smaller than the subheadings. Try to limit your fonts to about three different sizes.

- Limit the use of CAPITALS as it can make text hard to read and can appear 'aggressive'.

- Keep the text style consistent throughout the presentation to provide continuity.

- Check that the font size used in the presentation will appear clearly on the equipment you are using. Create an overhead transparency or slide and test it.

- Only use numbered paragraphs if your points have a specific order, otherwise use bullets to place equal importance on each paragraph.

- Use short sentences and statements. You can always give the audience a handout that details more information.

- Try using drop shadows to make interesting headings.

Exercise 66

What is wrong with the slide below?

....

....

....

Colour

- Use contrasting colours between text and background to make text easier to read.

- Use colour sparingly – try not to create a rainbow effect.

- Bright colours can be used to attract the viewer's attention to a particular topic/area.

- Use colour that is in keeping with the topic and tone of the presentation.

- Avoid colour combinations that are hard to read, eg blue/black, brown/green, red/green, blue/purple, yellow/white, brown/black.

Some colours evoke particular feelings – consider whether these are appropriate!

Red can indicate alertness, loss of earnings (financially) and excitement.

White represents professionalism, a sense of innocence and newness.

Blue represents reliability, trust and justice.

Black invokes authority and strength.

Green is used to stimulate and grow.

Orange promotes optimism and action.

Yellow indicates warmth, confidence and wisdom.

Brown is friendly and warm.

Grey indicates integrity and maturity.

Purple is used to add dignity and sophistication.

Pictures, Charts, Objects, Logos, etc

- Add clear pictures that are scaled and sized correctly.

- If adding an organisation's logo, insert it in the background at an appropriate location so it can appear on all slides.

- When using charts, apply contrasting colours with emphasis on the data to be discussed.

- Ensure a picture/object does not detract from the text if the text is to be the emphasis.

- Keep drawings/diagrams clear and concise.

- Limit the number of pictures, diagrams, etc on a slide as too many can appear cluttered.

- If using arrows ensure that they are pointing towards the appropriate object and that objects are aligned correctly.

- Ensure the pictures/objects relate to the topic of the slide.

- Use a variety of objects on different slides to keep interest, eg on one slide add a picture, on another add a diagram or drawing, etc.

- If using tables, apply the same font throughout the table.

- When inserting a pie chart, try to keep the number of slices to a maximum of six. Any more, and they can become hard to identify.

- Use a defined colour for a slice of a pie chart that is to be discussed. Position the slice on the slide so the presenter can easily point to it if required.

- If using a bar chart ensure the number of data series is limited, as too many series can make the chart unreadable.

- When using a line chart try to limit the number of lines to five or less. Too many lines and the reader may not be able to follow a particular line in the chart.

- Use colour and line thickness to distinguish the different data series in a line chart.

- When setting up the axis of a chart, ensure logical divisions are set based on the data series displayed.

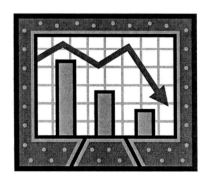

Sketch out your Presentation

It is a good idea to sketch out on a piece of paper the layout and order in which you wish to present information. The following is an example.

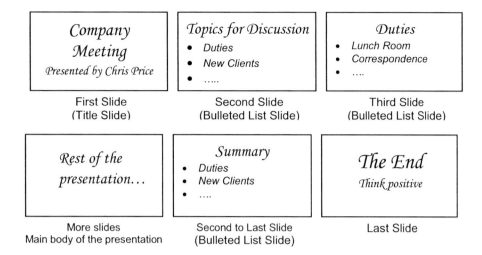

Use a Presentation Worksheet

If you have trouble sketching a presentation, a form may be helpful. An example is shown below. You may photocopy the form on the following two pages.

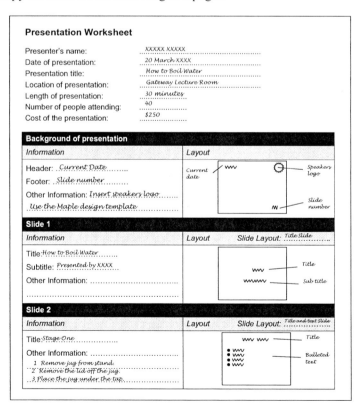

Presentation Worksheet

Presenter's name: ....
Date of presentation: ....
Presentation title: ....
Location of presentation: ....
Length of presentation: ....
Number of people attending: ....
Cost of presentation: ....

Background of presentation	
Information	*Layout*
Header: .... Footer: .... Other Information:	

Slide ☐	
Information	*Layout* Slide Layout: ....
Title: .... Subtitle: .... Other Information:	

Slide ☐	
Information	*Layout* Slide Layout: ....
Title: .... Other Information:	

Slide ▢

Information	Layout	Slide Layout: ....
Title: .... Other Information:		▢

Slide ▢

Information	Layout	Slide Layout: ....
Title: .... Other Information:		▢

Slide ▢

Information	Layout	Slide Layout: ....
Title: .... Other Information:		▢

Slide ▢

Information	Layout	Slide Layout: ....
Title: .... Other Information:		▢

1   Complete the following paragraph using the keywords given. (*Keywords*: projector, present, handouts, PowerPoint 2002, audience, slides)

    .... is a software program designed to help .... information to an .... The information presented could be in the form of ...., overhead transparencies, ... or slides using a ....

2   When costing a presentation what items should you take into account?

    ....

    ....

3   Explain why you would not use the colour combination blue/black.

    ....

    ....

4   Before your audience arrives what should you check in regard to the room/location of your presentation?

    ....

    ....

5   What type of slide would normally appear at the beginning of a presentation?

    ....

    ....

In the next set of exercises you will view a PowerPoint presentation, then create your own presentation for a Care Cosmetics managers' meeting.

Start PowerPoint

➤   Open Microsoft PowerPoint from the All Programs menu on the Start button, or click on the PowerPoint icon on your Desktop.

View a Presentation

1   Click on the Open button 📂 .

2   Double click on the file named 📇 North Sydney Arts Centre Presentation in the My Documents folder.

    The PowerPoint presentation will open with the first slide displayed.

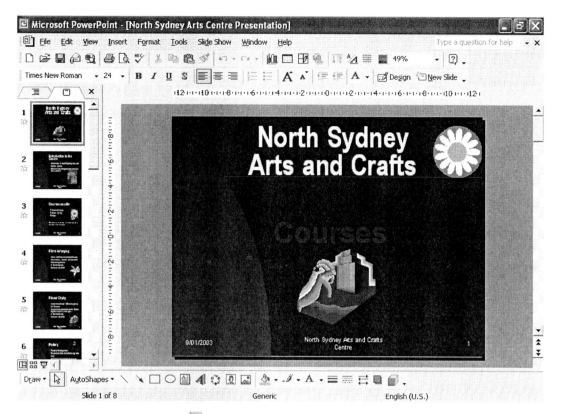

3   Click on Next Slide button ⬇ at the bottom right corner of the screen to display the next slide in the presentation.

4   Click on the Next Slide button repeatedly to move through all eight slides in the presentation.

5   Click on the Previous Slide button ⬆ to move backwards through the presentation.

6   Press Ctrl Home to return to the first slide.

7   Click on the Slide Sorter View button ⊞ at the bottom left of the screen to display all slides. Slides can be rearranged by clicking and dragging them to a new position.

8   Click on the Normal View button ⊞ to return to the previous view.

9   Click on the Slide Show button ⬜ to display the slide in full screen view; this is the view used when delivering a presentation to an audience.

10   Click the left mouse button to move to the next slide OR press the Page Down key.

     (Some slides are animated and you will need to click the mouse or press the Page Down key several times to move through all the text or graphics on the slide.)

11   At the end of the presentation, click the left mouse button to return to the PowerPoint screen automatically.

12   Close the presentation by choosing [File] Close.

Create a New Presentation

1   Click on the New button 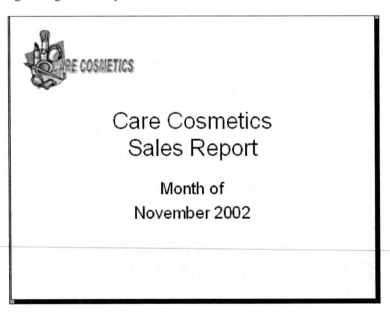. A new, blank presentation is created, with a Title slide displayed.
2   Click on the text *Click to add title*. Type: **Care Cosmetics** and press Enter, then type: **Sales Report**
3   Click on the text *Click to add subtitle*. Type: **Month of** and press Enter, then type **November 2002**
4   Click on the Save button .
5   Type: **Care Cosmetics Sales Report**
6   Click on Save.

Copy and Paste a Logo

In order to meet Care Cosmetics' organisational requirements for presentations, the company logo must be added to the Title slide.

1   Choose [Insert] Picture, From File
2   Click on the **Care Cosmetics Logo** file in My Documents folder, and click on Insert.
3   Click and drag the logo to the top left corner of the slide.

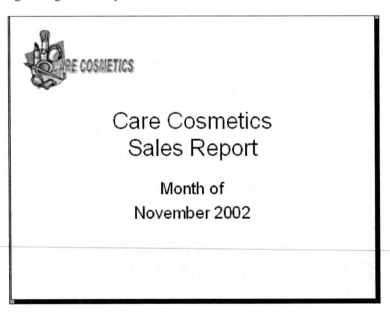

4   Save the changes to the presentation.

Create a Bulleted List Slide

Exercise 72

1   Click on ⌐New Slide ▾ to add a new slide to the presentation. Ensure the Title and Text format option is selected in the Task Pane.

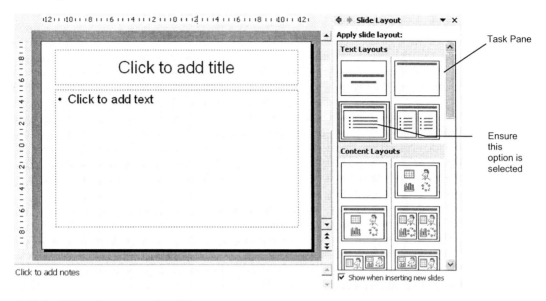

2   Add the following text to the slide.

Focus of November Sales

- Basic range of skin care products
- Skin care products related to sun care and aging
- Makeup with natural ingredients – supplied to the retail and wholesale markets
- Natural hair care products

3   Save the presentation.

Copy and Paste a Chart

A new slide is required in the presentation to show the sales results for the month of November.

Exercise 73

1   Add a new slide to the presentation, choosing the Title Only slide ⬜ format from the Task Pane.

2   Add the title: **November Sales**

3   Launch Microsoft Excel.

4   Open the workbook named **Care Cosmetics Sales** that you created in exercises 59 to 62.

5   Click on the pie chart in the November Sales worksheet to select it.

Ctrl C   6   Click on the Copy button 📋.

7   Click on the PowerPoint icon on the Taskbar to return to PowerPoint.

Ctrl V   8   Click on the Paste button 📋.

9   Resize and position the chart to display it appropriately on the slide.

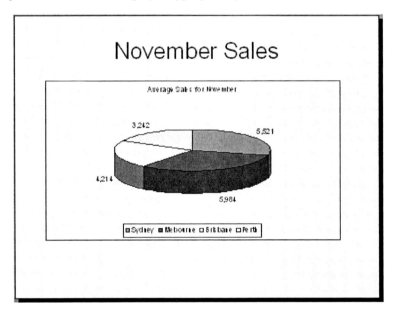

10   Save the presentation.

11   Return to Excel, close the workbook without saving changes and exit Excel.

Use Design Templates and Transitions

To enhance the presentation, colour and transitions may be added.

Exercise 74

1   Press Ctrl Home to move to the first slide.

2   Choose [Format] Slide Design.

3   Click on the Blends option in the Apply a design template: section of the Task Pane (if you place your cursor over an option, its name will be displayed).

Move the logo if it obscures the text

4   Click on the Slide Sorter View button ⊞ at the bottom left of the screen.

5   Check the layout of slide 3. If the chart is obscuring the design, click on slide 3 and resize the chart. Then click on the Slide Sorter View button again.

6   Ensure Slide 1 is selected and choose [Slide Show] Slide Transition.

7   Click on Box Out in the *Apply to selected slides*: section of the Task Pane.

8   Add the following transitions to Slides 2 and 3.

     Slide 2   Cover Down

     Slide 3   Wipe Up

9   Click on Slide 1 then save the changes.

10   Click on the Slide Show button ⊡ to run the presentation.

11   Click the left mouse button to move through the slides.

12   Choose [File] Close to close the presentation.

Exercise 75

You have been asked to present the information gathered about mobile phone packages for staff at Care Cosmetics, including explaining why the phones are needed, and any relevant background information.

Resources to help:

- *Scenario at the beginning of the book.*
- *Mobile phones scenario on pages 5 and 6.*
- *Information collected in Exercise 5.*

1   Create a plan outlining the steps required to create the presentation and include a cost outline. Explain what tools you will use and the reason for using them.

2 Fill in the gaps below for the presentation.

Presentation Topic: ....

Purpose of presentation: ....

Target Audience: ....

Date of Presentation: ....

Length of Presentation (time): ....

3 Gather the information you need and put it in a logical order.

4 Sketch out your presentation using a copy of the Presentation Worksheet on pages 108 and 109.

5 Create the presentation in PowerPoint.

6 Check your presentation against the first part of the Presentation Check List (Creating a presentation) on page 118.

Deliver a Presentation

The following points will assist in delivering a professional, polished presentation.

- Practise your presentation on your PC (if required) more than twice. Then rehearse in front of another person.

- If using a microphone, understand its limits and use. Always test before the audience appears.

- Test the equipment and do a run through before the presentation starts (dress rehearsal).

- Check the room environment – lighting, temperature, outside noise, enough seating, etc.

- Ensure that your presentation is visible to all of the audience.

- When using equipment for the first time, make sure you know how to use it and that your presentation works effectively before you begin presenting.

- Ensure the lights are on when introducing yourself. You can dim lights once you are underway but ensure as a presenter you can be seen by the audience.

- Beware of starting with a joke – if it falls flat your confidence will take a severe beating.

- Try not to stand in one place on the floor or hide behind a podium unless you have a static microphone. Ensure the audience can see you and remember that a bit of movement can reawaken an audience.

- Check your movements are appropriate (not too much hand movement, not rocking back and forth) when presenting. Too much movement can become a distraction.

- Body language plays an important part in any presentation - learn to think about how you use your eyes, legs and hands when speaking and referencing your slides or transparencies. Use your hands to convey normal body actions as if you were in ordinary conversation.

- If using overhead transparencies or slides ensure they are in the correct order.

- Make sure you have clear presentation objectives when introducing a presentation and that all those objectives are met.

- Be enthusiastic when presenting a topic. This will encourage the audience to listen.

- Make eye contact with your audience when presenting.

- Stay on the topic.

- Think about including audience involvement in your presentation. This is good when starting a presentation or in the middle of a presentation, as it attracts the audience's attention.

- When pointing to an item on an overhead transparency ensure you point to the actual transparency instead of the screen, to avoid blocking the light with your body.

- Most speakers use notes but do not read directly from these - it is important to make eye contact with your audience. You may feel more comfortable memorising some of your notes but try not to deliver your presentation purely by memory. Use pauses in your speech and avoid the common "verbal pauses" such as "umm" and "okay".

- When ending a presentation ensure that you have a closure, eg "That concludes my presentation on ……..", so that everyone knows you have finished.

- Always have a backup plan in case equipment breaks down, eg overhead projector blows a bulb, the computer attached to the projector crashes, etc.

- Be early, organised and know your presentation.

Navigate in a PowerPoint Presentation

Keyboard

Click on the Slide Show button and use the following keys

Action	Key
Next Slide	Page Down
Previous Slide	Page Up
Move to the Last Slide in the Presentation	Ctrl End
Move to the First Slide	Ctrl Home

Mouse

Action	Mouse
Next Slide	Left click
Previous Slide	Right click and choose Previous

Exercise 76

1   Practise the navigation options above in the presentation you created in Exercise 75.

2   Rehearse the presentation.

3   When you are ready, present the information to a classmate.

4   Check your presentation technique against the Evaluation Check List on page 118.

5   Close your file saving any changes, and exit PowerPoint.

Evaluation Check List

Use the following check list to check your efficiency in preparing and delivering your presentation.

	Points to consider	Checked
Creating a presentation	Is the information concise? (You can talk and hand out more comprehensive notes if required.)	
	Is the presentation simple? Too much text and graphics on the page can seem daunting.	
	Will the audience be focused on the correct information, or on the fancy graphic in the corner of my slide?	
	Are there too many animation effects? Will this distract the audience?	
	Does the presentation have direction, focus, information and reinforcement?	
	Are there handouts? If so, do they contain detailed information about the presentation?	
Before delivering a presentation	Have I practised delivering the presentation?	
	Do I have a backup plan if I cannot run the slide show or slides?	
	Do I know my presentation tools - slide projector, overhead transparency projector, data projector, laser pointer, remote mouse, etc?	
	Has all the equipment I am going to use been tested?	
	Is the room is set up correctly, ready for my presentation?	
	Do I know my presentation topic well?	
	Am I ready to present?	
Presenting	Did I present to my audience, not my computer, projector or white/blackboard?	
	Did I watch out for "umm", "ahh" and "okay".	
	Did I answer questions either as they occurred OR state that I would answer questions at the end of the presentation? Did I ensure I left time for questions?	
	Was I aware of my body language?	
At the end of the presentation	Did I thank the audience?	
	Did I make handouts, etc, available?	
	Did I make myself available?	
	Did I obtain feedback?	

Other Methods of Conveying Information

While PowerPoint may be the perfect tool to use when presenting information to a group, there will be many occasions on which you will need to convey information to a group of people who are not located in the same place. There are a number of useful ways to communicate with others in this type of situation, and many of these have been covered in this book. Your word processing package can produce a huge range of documents, beyond standard letters and memos, to convey information in an informative and attractive manner.

Reports

A report is often written by senior members of a firm or organisation; it sets out facts and conclusions and can be printed on letterhead or plain paper. Some reports are very involved, and some simple, but most take into account the following points.

- There should be a heading, and the word REPORT is often included as part of it.

- A report should have an introductory paragraph, and a final paragraph which contains conclusions and/or recommendations.

- The writer's name, or the company name, is inserted either as part of the heading, at the foot of the document or on the title page of the report.

- The report must be dated.

Layout

The layout of a report can vary from single column to multi-column. Reports require consistency and continuity throughout and this must be reflected in the layout.

An example of a complex report is shown below.

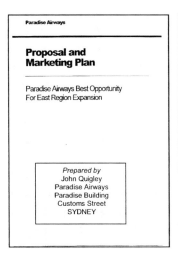

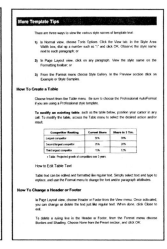

Faxes

In the following exercises a standard fax form will be created for Care Cosmetics. This template will be used to create a fax message containing spreadsheet data and a chart of the sales results.

Note The following exercise is also completed in the book *Produce Business Documents – BSBCMN306A*; if you have completed this book, you will be able to use your completed fax template and will not need to complete exercise 77.

Create a Fax Form Template

Codes can be used with *fillin* commands in templates to ensure that data is entered efficiently. Prompt boxes will be displayed in which you can enter information, as shown at the right.

Exercise 77

1   Launch Word.

2   In a new document create the fax form shown below, inserting the logo, contact details and heading text, eg To:, Company: etc. Insert the date field as instructed on the form.

Insert the *fillin* fields using the following instructions:

3   Move to the position of the first field code (ie after **To:** →) and Press Ctrl F9 to insert the field code brackets.

4   Type: **fillin** followed by a space, then the message, in quotation marks, that should appear in the prompt box, eg **{ fillin "Who is this fax to?" }**. Remember to end the quotation marks.

5   Press End to move outside the field brackets. Repeat to insert all the fillin codes.

CARE COSMETICS

Brisbane Branch, 200 Alice Street, Brisbane, Queensland 4000
Ph (07) 3452 4391   Fax (07) 3452 4392

Facsimile

To:	{ fillin "Who is this fax to?" }
Company:	{ fillin "Company Name" }
Fax No:	{ fillin "Fax number" }
From:	{ fillin "Who is this fax from" }
Date:	(Choose [Insert] Field, Date and Time, choose the Date field name, select a format and click on OK.)
Subject:	{ fillin "Subject of fax" }
Number of Pages: (incl. cover)	{ fillin "No. of pages" }

---

1   Click on the Save button.

2   Type: **Care Cosmetics Fax** in the File name: box.

3   Click on the Save as type: ▾ and select Document Template.

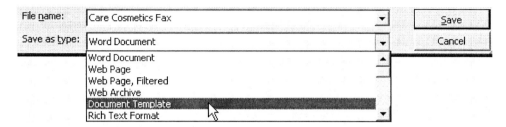

4   Click on Save.

5   Close the document.

Use the Fax Template

Exercise 78

1   Choose [File] New.

2   Click on General Templates in the Task Pane.

3   From the General tab of the Templates dialog box, double click on the **Care Cosmetics Fax** to open a new document based on the template. The first prompt box will be displayed.

New from template
    Client Diary Note
    External Writer Diary Note
    General Templates...
    Templates on my Web Sites...
    Templates on Microsoft.com

4   Type: **Alan Carter** in the prompt box.

5   Click on OK OR press Tab then Enter to move to the next prompt box.

6   Continue entering the information shown below into each prompt box using the above steps. Then type the message text.

TO: Alan Carter

COMPANY: Care Cosmetics, Head Office

FAX: 94-29 8325

FROM: Kevin Thompson

DATE: (Today's)

SUBJECT: November Sales Spreadsheet

NO. OF PAGES: 1

The sales figures below were provided to us at the last branch managers' meeting, but I don't believe they are correct. Would you please check against your own records and advise me if you find any discrepancies for Brisbane branch's results?

---

7   Save as **Fax – Alan Carter.**

Copy and Paste Information into a Fax Message

Exercise 79

Ctrl O

1   Launch Excel.

2   Click on the Open button 🖝 OR choose [File] Open.

3   Double click on the file named **Care Cosmetics Sales** to open it.

4   Select cells A1 to F11.

	A	B	C	D	E	F
1	**Care Cosmetics**					
2	November Sales					
3						
4		*Week 1*	*Week 2*	*Week 3*	*Week 4*	*Average Sales*
5						
6	Sydney	5,612	4,587	5,874	6,012	5,521
7	Melbourne	6,566	5,644	5,987	5,740	5,984
8	Brisbane	4,422	3,754	4,671	4,007	4,214
9	Perth	2,886	2,950	3,520	3,610	3,242
10						
11	Total	$19,486	$16,935	$20,052	$19,369	$18,961

Ctrl C

5   Click on the Copy button 📋 OR choose [Edit] Copy.

6   Click on the Word icon on the Taskbar to return to the document named **Fax – Alan Carter**.

7   Press Ctrl End to ensure your cursor is at the end of the document, and press Enter twice.

8   Click on the Paste button 📋 to add the spreadsheet to your document as a Word table.

Format a Pasted Spreadsheet

Exercise 80

1   Click anywhere in the column heading row (Week 1, Week 2…).

2   Choose [Table] Split Table.

3   Click in the second table.

4   Choose [Table] Table AutoFormat.

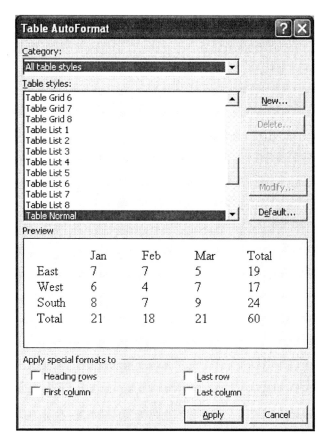

Table AutoFormat

Category:

All table styles

Table styles:

Table Grid 6
Table Grid 7
Table Grid 8
Table List 1
Table List 2
Table List 3
Table List 4
Table List 5
Table List 6
Table List 7
Table List 8
Table Normal

New...
Delete...
Modify...
Default...

Preview

	Jan	Feb	Mar	Total
East	7	7	5	19
West	6	4	7	17
South	8	7	9	24
Total	21	18	21	60

Apply special formats to

☐ Heading rows   ☐ Last row
☐ First column   ☐ Last column

Apply   Cancel

5   Click on different formats in the Table styles: section to preview formatting options.

6   Select a format of your choice (not one with too much shading because it won't transmit well through a fax machine) then click on Apply.

Note To adjust column widths if required, double click on the vertical border between two columns.

7   Save the changes to the document.

Copy and Paste Excel Charts

Exercise 81

1   In the fax document, add the following text beneath the table:

The bar chart that was also provided is shown below.

2   Press Enter twice.

3   Click on the Excel icon on the Taskbar to return to the workbook named **Care Cosmetics Sales**.

4   Click on the **November Sales Chart** worksheet tab.

5   Click in the white area to the left of the chart title to select the chart.

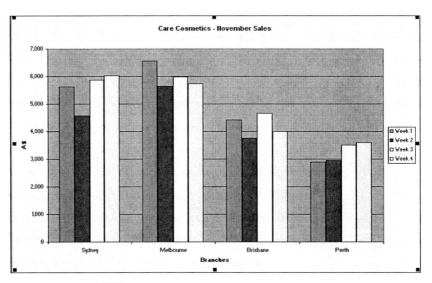

6 Click on the Copy button .

7 Return to the Word document named **Fax – Alan Carter**.

8 Click on the Paste button to add the chart to the fax document.

9 If necessary, click and drag on the sizing handles to fit the chart on the same page as the rest of the document.

Sizing Handles

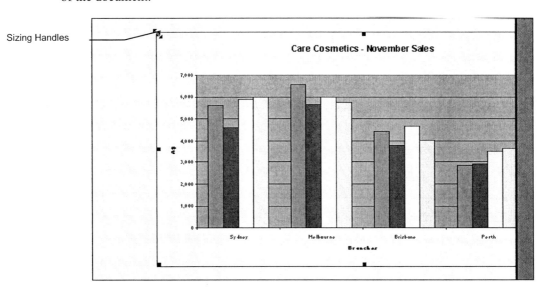

10 Return to Excel. Close the workbook and Excel without saving any changes.

11 Print, save and close the fax document in Word, then exit Word.

Communicate Information to Designated Persons

In order to communicate information appropriately to the correct people, you must first have an understanding of the "chain of command" in your organisation. Part of this will be official, and you should expect that there will also be unwritten rules about the hierarchy of staff and positions.

Organisation Chart

Depending on the size and type of organisation the roles of staff will vary. The following organisational chart shows an example of the flow of authority and responsibility, from the Board of Directors (overall control) to the Receptionist.

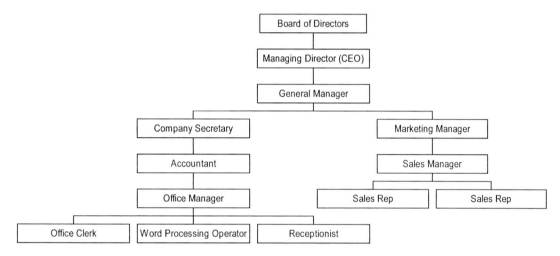

Lines of Communication

Lines of communication are the channels through which people communicate. A line of communication may include **people**, **things**, and **events**. For example:

- If the best way to get a message to your boss is to speak to her chauffeur, then the **chauffeur** is a line of communication to your boss.

- If the best way to let your department know the latest news is through the department newsletter, then the **newsletter** is a line of communication to people in your department.

- If the best way to find out what the sales people think about your new product is through the six-monthly sales conference, then the **conference** is your line of communication to the sales people.

Lines of communication can be:

- Oral or written
- Informal or formal
- Direct or indirect

Take a look at these examples.

Example: Line of communication between you and a close colleague

Your line of communication to a colleague who sits 10 metres away will probably be:

- Oral (you will speak to him)
- Informal (because you will probably know him quite well)
- Direct (without using any other person or equipment)

Example: Line of communication between you and the prime minister

However, if you wanted to contact the prime minister (assuming he's not a great pal of yours), you would probably need to communicate in **writing**, because you would not be able to get close enough to speak to him. You would communicate **formally**, because he is somebody you do not know personally. Your line of communication would also be **indirect,** because your letter would be dealt with by a secretary or assistant acting as a **go-between**.

In summary, your line of communication with the prime minister would be

- Written
- Formal
- Indirect

Use Go-betweens

In large organisations you won't be able to communicate with everyone directly; instead you will use others as go-betweens.

Some people are specifically responsible for communicating and acting as go-betweens. For instance, a manager may have a secretary whose job it is to communicate on behalf of her boss, and to act as a go-between so that the boss's time is used effectively.

If people have specific responsibility for acting as a go-between, then make sure you go to them when you need to pass on, or receive, information for which they are responsible.

Factors Influencing Lines of Communication

Lines of communication will depend on a number of factors, including the following.

Authority

Who has authority within the organisation to make announcements, tell people what to do, or enforce rules?

The following exercise explores this issue.

Exercise 82

Danny works in a restaurant. His supervisor, the restaurant manager, has asked him to come up with a set of rules for all the kitchen staff, to ensure they keep food and equipment clean, and observe health and hygiene regulations.

Danny has produced a set of rules, and realises that it is very important that his colleagues should know and follow them. However, he also knows that he does not have the authority to tell the kitchen staff what to do. Should he:

(a) Pin the rules to a notice board and hope that the kitchen staff notice them?

(b) Strut around the kitchen, waving his new rulebook around and loudly explaining how important they are?

(c) Ask the restaurant manager to inform the kitchen staff of the new rules, and explain their importance?

Your answer: ....

Explain the reason for your answer.

....

....

....

Seniority

Some organisations are strict about who you can or cannot communicate directly with. For instance, if you are a corporal in the army, you can't just march up to a Brigadier General to complain that your helmet is the wrong size.

If you need to communicate with someone senior in an organisation, or someone who tends to be very busy:

• Find out whether there is someone you should use as a go-between. This might be their secretary or assistant, or someone who works for them.

• If they do not have a secretary, try emailing them to ask for an appointment to speak to them at a convenient time.

Proximity

How close is the person with whom you need to communicate?

Sometimes you will need to communicate with people who are not immediately available to you. You might not even know who they are.

If you need to communicate with people in other locations, you might need to use indirect lines of communication. This might involve:

• Writing to them, either by post or electronic mail.

• Telephoning them.

• Using somebody else as a go-between. For instance, if you need to communicate with people in another building, you might speak first to the receptionist in that building.

Exercise 83

Debbie's company has changed its prices for a list of products, and her supervisor has asked her to let the sales representatives know (there are 15 of them). They all work from home, in different parts of the country. Their supervisor, the Sales Manager, works in the same office as Debbie. The Sales Manager produces a Daily Bulletin that is mailed to each sales representative to keep them informed of new developments.

Should Debbie:

(a) Hire a car and visit each sales representative at home, to ensure they get the message?

(b) Call a meeting for all the sales representatives, so that she can read out the new prices to them?

(c) Speak to the Sales Manager, and ask what she thinks is the best way to let the sales representatives know?

Your answer: ....

Explain the reason for your answer.

....

....

....

The number of people you need to communicate with

Is it impractical or inappropriate for you to communicate with many people at once?

In Debbie's case there were several reasons why it was appropriate to approach the Sales Manager, one of which was that it was impractical for her to approach so many people individually.

If you need to communicate with a large number of people, you could:

- Write a memorandum, and post it to each person.

- Send an email message.

- Hold a meeting.

- Make an announcement over a public address system.

- Use a go-between who has direct, or regular, contact with the people with whom you need to communicate.

Exercise 84

Minnie works at a police station. She needs to let all the front-line officers know that new batons have arrived to replace the existing ones, which are now obsolete.

Minnie does not know the names of all the front-line officers, but she knows they should all be using their new batons by the end of the week.

She also knows that the Sergeants debrief front-line staff at the beginning of every shift.

Should Minnie:

(a) Stand at the gates of the police station, rattling a box of batons and shouting, "Get your batons here!"?

(b) Leave a box of batons on reception and hope that all the front-line officers notice?

(c) Ask the shift Sergeants to act as go-betweens and announce during debriefing that the new batons are ready for collection?

Your answer: ....

Explain the reason for your answer.

....

....

....

Sensitive information

Sometimes, information is sensitive or confidential.

For instance, if you worked as a filing clerk in a hospital and found out that a patient's test results were back and it had been discovered that he was very sick, you would be in possession of sensitive and confidential information. You would not talk to the patient about his test results directly. You would pass the information to the appropriate doctor or nurse, and that person would deal with the patient.

Certain information between colleagues at work is similarly confidential. For instance, information relating to a person's salary, terms and conditions of employment, and career prospects are generally regarded as sensitive subjects, and are often confidential.

In the case of sensitive or confidential information, there are often strict rules governing what you can and cannot do, and what the lines of communication should be.

Exercise 85

Based on the Care Cosmetics sales information scenario, draw an organisation chart (on the next page) that reflects the organisation as it existed before the changes that have occurred over the past year.

Draw a second chart illustrating the current likely/possible structure.

Compare the two charts. What lines of communication would you have used to communicate sales information based on the first organisation chart? How would you communicate based on the changes reflected in the second chart?

Care Cosmetics Organisation Chart 1 (Prior to Changes)

Care Cosmetics Organisation Chart 2 (After Changes)

Notes

....
....
....
....
....
....
....
....
....
....
....
....

Difficulties in Accessing and Organising Information

The process of managing information may produce a wide range of issues. You may have difficulties obtaining the information you need, or be unable or unsure how to organise or convey the information. In this section you will review some of these issues and how they can be resolved.

Communication Issues

Many problems surrounding the correct collection, organisation and use of information come about through poor communication. A poor choice of method of collecting, organising or presenting information, or poor interpersonal skills, are likely possibilities. Consider the following points.

Computers versus People

When is a computer more appropriate than a person for carrying out a task – and when not?

Would you really like to see a computerised robot sitting at a reception desk? The only time it could answer your questions would be when the actual question was already programmed into it with a response. Computers could not therefore replace a front-desk person effectively.

Exercise 86

Complete the following table, creating a list of tasks best completed by a person, and a second list of tasks best suited to a computer. Ensure you have three items in each list and briefly explain the reasons for your choice in each example.

	Task best suited to a person	Task best suited to a computer	Why?
1			
2			
3			

Answering the Telephone

Many people get annoyed with computerised answering systems which request you to press one key to access a menu, then another key, etc, and some hang up out of sheer frustration. While most people would probably prefer to communicate with a telephone operator, there will always be some who like the automation of the computerised system.

Teamwork

If boundaries and responsibilities are not set right at the beginning, someone with a dominant personality can tend to influence other team members to the detriment of the team, or two dominant personalities may clash. If the team is small (three people), two team members may form an alliance, excluding the third member.

High levels of negativity and passivity among team members will destroy the group process. There can be individual resistance to working in teams. This must be recognised and training given to the individual(s) who prefer to work in isolation, or those individuals should not be included in the team.

Everyone must agree on milestones and deadlines. If one of the team members is a procrastinator he or she will delay the rest of the team. On the other hand, if someone does not meet a deadline it could be that they have an unacceptable workload, and this will have to be re-assessed by the team.

It is important that team members possess the skills required to complete the task. Technical skills are particularly important, and it could be necessary to co-opt additional members to the team in order to cope with technical requirements.

Sometimes a lack of skills is not discovered until the project is under way, and then it can be difficult to assimilate new members into the team.

Negative past experiences about teamwork may influence people in future teams. This has to be discussed and steps taken to avoid a repetition of the negative experience.

Review Processes

If you believe your problem does not lie specifically with a communication or interpersonal skills issue, you must review the *processes* you have used to manage the information.

- How was the information collected? Were the method(s) chosen appropriate for the type of information being collected?

- Was the correct information requested? Were the requirements made clear?

- Was the information collated logically?

- Has the correct equipment, technology and format been used to organise the information?

These questions should allow you to identify problems associated with accessing and organising information.

Resolve the Problem

The review process may clarify not only where the problem lies, but also show clearly what must be changed to resolve it. Sometimes, the answer may not be so clear, and you may need to access other resources to find an effective solution.

Seek Assistance

People such as your supervisor, mentor, a trainer or colleagues may be able to provide you with information about how to achieve your objectives.

Some colleagues will be more willing and able to help than others. Seek out colleagues who have one or more of the following attributes.

- Skills and experience relevant to the task you are completing.
- Responsibility for training you or providing you with information.
- A helpful attitude.

If you work in a very large organisation, it might employ Human Resources managers, trainers, librarians, information officers, or other experts whose function it is to assist staff to gain knowledge and information.

Refer to Books and Manuals

You may find books and manuals that could throw some light on the problem. These could be found:

In the offices, or workspaces, of appropriate people. For instance, a guide to writing a marketing plan would be with the marketing manager.

On bookshelves in shared spaces. Your organisation might have bookshelves in corridors, meeting rooms, the reception area, or other shared space. Do not forget to check these for useful information.

In the library. Some organisations have their own libraries. If yours does not, and you need a book for reference or to help you develop skills, then consider visiting the nearest public library, or a specialist library catering for your industry.

On the organisation's Intranet. More and more organisations are placing manuals and guide books on their intranet systems (a private section of the Internet). If your organisation has an intranet, then make sure you use it. Take some time to get to know it. If you don't know how to use it, then get someone to show you. Intranets normally have vast amounts of information that is specific to the needs of an organisation.

Complete a Training Course

For complex tasks it might be appropriate for you to attend training sessions, or training courses, to learn how to do them properly, or how to use the tools you have effectively.

Use your Computer Support Desk

It is sometimes more efficient to use the services of a Help Desk Operator than to try and find your way around some computerised Help systems. A problem can be out of the range of the help offered on a computer system whereas an operator usually has access to an extensive database and also has personal knowledge.

Research the Problem on the Internet

The World Wide Web consists of the millions of pages that can be viewed when you access the Internet. It contains massive amounts of information, some of which will be useful to you at work. If you do not know how to use the Internet, ask someone to show you. Use search engines to target the areas that are of interest to you.

Check Walls and Notice Boards

Sometimes, in our quest for information, we don't see what's in front of our eyes. To make information easy to find, some organisations pin it to the wall. Don't forget to look at notice boards to find guidelines and instructions. If you are using equipment, the instructions might be pinned to the wall near where equipment is stored or operated.

Exercise 87

The rapid expansion of Care Cosmetics branches and satellite sites has resulted in a general feeling of dissatisfaction about the access to collated sales results from head office. The results are sometimes received several weeks after they have been collated, and sometimes not at all! Consider the points discussed on pages 131 to 134 and note any possible solutions to this problem.

....

....

....

....

....

....

....

....

....

....

....

....

....

....

....

....

....

....

....

Section

4

Store Information

Learning Outcomes

At the end of this section you should be able to -

❑   Use electronic storage options.

❑   Use storage options for paper-based records.

Store Information Electronically

As computer files continue to become an accepted method of information storage, electronic file management skills take on a greater importance than ever before. Information flows into organisations at an increasingly high rate, and it is important to have the tools and skills to store this information in a logical electronic file management system.

There are many types of applications that will make up a typical computer-based storage system in an organisation. These include:

- File management applications (eg Windows Explorer)
- Personal Information Managers, referred to as PIMs (eg Outlook)
- Project management applications (eg MS Project)
- Database applications (eg Access)
- Spreadsheet applications (eg Excel)

In this section, you will learn how to use Windows Explorer to establish a logical folder structure, and how to use one aspect of Outlook (Email) to store incoming information.

Use Windows Explorer

Windows Explorer is Microsoft's file management application, and is an integrated part of the MS Windows operating system.

Exercise 88

1 Right click on **start** on the Windows Desktop and select Explore.

2 Choose [View] Tiles to ensure the icons are displayed as shown below.

(Files on your computer will be different.)

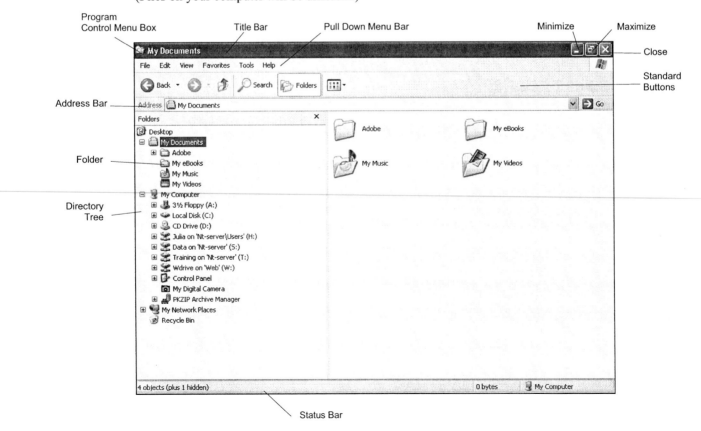

© Software Educational Resources Ltd

Program Control Menu Box

The Program Control Menu Box is used to maximise, minimise or close Windows Explorer.

Title Bar

The Title Bar is located at the top of the Window, and displays the name of the program.

Menu Bar

The menu bar provides access to Windows Explorer commands.

Minimize and Maximize

These buttons are used to increase (maximise) and decrease (minimise to an icon) the size of the main Windows Explorer window.

Close

Closes the Windows Explorer window, exiting Windows Explorer.

Standard Buttons

A toolbar that provides fast access to commonly-used commands.

Address Bar

Displays the location of the current folder/drive selected.

Folder

Provides storage for files.

Folder Structure/Directory Tree

Displays the structure and location of folders and files on your computer.

Status Bar

Displays information about the current file/folder/drive selected.

Windows Explorer Toolbars

There are three toolbars in Windows Explorer – Standard Buttons, Address Bar and Links.

Standard Buttons Toolbar

Buttons	Name	Menu Option	Description
Back ▾	Back	[View] Go To, Back	Displays the last position/view.
▾	Forward	[View] Go To, Forward	If you had just clicked on Back you could click on Forward to move to the position/view you were originally viewing.
	Up	[View] Go To, Up One Level	Moves up one folder in the structure.
Search	Search	[View] Explorer Bar, Search	Displays the Search bar at the left of Windows Explorer, where you can search for files and folders.
Folders	Folders	[View] Explorer Bar, Folders	Displays the Folders bar at the left of Windows Explorer, showing the structure and location of folders and files.
▾	Views	[View]	Choose from different view options that change the way you view files/folders.

The buttons on the Standard Buttons bar may appear as small icons with no text labels.

Text labels can be added to buttons by choosing [View] Toolbars, Customize, Text options. The size of icons can also be changed in this dialog box.

Turn On/Off Toolbars

Toolbars can be turned on/off by either of the following methods.

- Choose [View] Toolbars. Select the toolbar required.
- Right click on a toolbar and select the toolbar required.

Folder Structure

The folder structure, also referred to as a Directory Tree, lies at the heart of any file management program. In Windows Explorer, the folder structure is viewed on the left side of the window.

A *file* may be a program file, such as those associated with Word and Excel, or a data file, such as the Word, Excel and PowerPoint files you have created throughout this book. For the purposes of storing information, we are primarily concerned with data files.

A *folder* is a place to store files – the electronic equivalent of a cardboard folder stored in a filing cabinet.

A *subfolder* refers to a folder that is contained within another folder, for the purpose of organising files into logical groups so that they may be easily located.

In the folder structure example shown at the right, the Adobe and Care Cosmetics folders are subfolders of My Documents. The four branch folders are subfolders of the Care Cosmetics folder.

Although there are "standard" folders, such as My Documents, which can be found on any Windows computer, other folders will be different from one computer to the next, depending on the structure created by the computer user.

- 🗁 My Documents
  - ⊞ 🗁 Adobe
  - ⊟ 🗁 Care Cosmetics
    - 🗁 Brisbane Branch
    - 🗁 Melbourne Branch
    - 🗁 Perth Branch
    - 🗁 Sydney Branch

Exercise 89

1   Locate and click on My Documents folder at the left of the Window.

Folders are represented by a yellow folder icon ☐. Click on a folder to open it ☐. The files contained in a folder that has been opened will be displayed at the right of the window, as is the case with My Documents folder that you have just opened.

A folder that contains subfolders will have a + or − symbol displayed next to it.

The + symbol next to a folder indicates that subfolders exist which aren't currently displayed in the folder structure on the left of the window (although they may be viewed on the right of the window).

To display subfolders, click on the + symbol; it changes to a − symbol, indicating that all subfolders are displayed.

2   Ensure the subfolders contained in My Documents folder are displayed.

3   Click on the Faxes folder. The files contained in the folder are displayed at the right of the window.

4   Click on the Budget folder to view the files contained in it.

Files

A file is a collection of data assigned to a name. As previously discussed, files can relate to programs that run on a computer, or they can be data files created by the computer user.

The program in which a data file was created can usually be identified by the icon located next to the file name.

You can double click on a data file to open both the file and the program in which it was created.

File Extensions

All files have the option to display an extension. An extension is used to identify the file type and can be between one and three characters long. It appears at the end of the file name. Files that Windows can identify do not normally display extensions. In Windows an icon is used to represent the file type, as mentioned above.

The file name at the left displays the file name **memo** and the extension **.doc**. The **.doc** extension is used to identify a document file created in Word.

Examples of file extensions are listed below.

Explorer.exe	Executable file (this type of file will start a program)
Win.com	
Readme.txt	Text file
Auckland Sales.xls	Excel file
Stock.mdb	Access file
Parrot.pcx	Picture file
Hat.tif	
Report.msg	Message file
Index.htm	Hypertext Markup file (web page)

Display/Hide File Extensions

Exercise 90

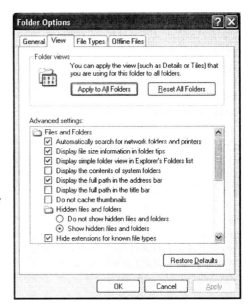

1   Choose [Tools] Folder Options. Click on the View tab.

2   Click in the *Hide extensions for known file types* check box to remove the tick. Click on OK.

With the Budget folder open, you can see the files displayed with their file extensions.

3   Choose [Tools] Folder Options. Click on the View tab.

4   Click on the *Hide extensions for known file types* check box. Click on OK.

Any files Windows can identify are shown without the extension. Windows will be able to recognise the files with which you commonly work – documents, presentations, spreadsheets, databases etc, and will not display the extension unless this option is selected.

View Files and Folders

There are many different ways of viewing files and folders.

Display Files

Exercise 91

1   Click on the Views button and select Details OR choose [View] Details to display a detailed list of files.

2   Click on the Views button and select List OR choose [View] List to display files as a list of file names.

3   Click on the Views button and select Icons OR choose [View] Icons to display files as icons.

4   Click on the Views button and select Thumbnails OR choose [View] Thumbnails to display a small preview of each file in the icon. (For this to happen, [File] Properties, Save Preview Picture option must be checked in the program of origin before the file was saved.)

Document with saved preview   Document with no saved preview   Image that can be previewed   Image that cannot be previewed

5   Click on the Views button and select Details OR choose [View] Details.

Arrange Files

Exercise 92

1   Click on My Documents folder.

2   Choose [View] Arrange Icons by. Icons can be arranged by Name, Size, Type or (Date) Modified.

3   Click on Modified. Files will be listed in the date order in which they were last saved.

   Note   Folders are always listed before files.

4   Choose [View] Arrange Icons by, Size. Files will be listed by file size, from smallest to largest.

5   View files arranged by Type, to see (for example) all Word files listed together, and all Excel files listed together.

6   View files arranged by Name to list them in alphabetical order.

Tip   Right click in the space at the right of a list of files to display a shortcut menu. From the Arrange Icons by option, files can be organised into the required order.

Create New Folders

Exercise 93

1   With My Documents folder open choose [File] New, Folder.

   A new folder is displayed in the list of files at the right of the window and the New Folder box is ready to enter the name of the new folder.

2   Type: **Exercise Disk** and press Enter.

Ctrl Z   If you make a mistake, choose [Edit] Undo.

   The folder named Exercise Disk will appear as a subfolder of My Documents in the folder structure at the left of the window.

3   With My Documents folder open, choose [File] New, Folder

4   Type: **Graphics** and press Enter.

   A new folder named Graphics will appear in My Documents folder.

A new folder will become a subfolder of the folder that is currently open. For example, to create a subfolder of My Documents, you must ensure that folder is open at the time the new folder is created.

Copy Files

Exercise 94

1   Click on the file named **hat** in My Documents folder. (You may need to scroll down the list of files using the Vertical Scroll bar.)

Ctrl C   2   Choose [Edit] Copy.

3   Click on the Graphics folder, which is the new location for the file.

Ctrl V   4   Choose [Edit] Paste.

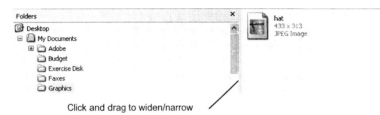

Click and drag to widen/narrow

 Tip An alternative to using the Clipboard (choosing [Edit] Copy) is to Ctrl click and drag selected files to a destination (folder or drive).

Select Files

Exercise 95

➤   Try selecting files in My Documents folder using the methods shown below.

Selecting a Single File
Click on the file ONCE.

Selecting a Random Group of Files
Click on the first file, hold down Ctrl and click on other files to select.

Selecting Adjacent Files
Click on the first file, move your mouse pointer (without holding down the mouse button) to the last file in the list. Hold down Shift and click on the file. All files between the two files will be selected.

Selecting All Files
Press Ctrl A OR choose [Edit] Select All.

Deselecting Files
Click anywhere to deselect all files, OR hold down Ctrl and click on individual files to be deselected.

Invert Selection

Inverting selected files means that they will be deselected, and those files not selected will be selected. This can be useful when you need to select most, but not all, files in a folder. Instead of selecting the many files you *do* want, select the few you *don't* want, then invert the selection.

1   Hold down Ctrl and click on files/folders you do not wish to select.

2   Choose [Edit] Invert Selection.

Move Files

There are two ways of moving a file – using the mouse, or the Clipboard ([Edit] Cut). The first exercise demonstrates use of the Clipboard.

Exercise 96

1   In the Faxes folder, select the file named **Office Supplies**

Ctrl X   2   Choose [Edit] Cut.

3   Click on the Budget folder.

Ctrl V   4   Choose [Edit] Paste.

Move Files Using the Mouse

Exercise 97

1   In the Budget folder, select the file named **Office Supplies**

2   Move your mouse pointer over the selected file.

3   Click and drag to the Faxes folder. (Ensure the Faxes folder is highlighted before releasing the left mouse button.)

> Note   Files can be copied in the same manner by holding down Ctrl when dragging.

Rename Files and Folders

Renaming a file will not alter the contents of the file; only the name itself will be changed.

Exercise 98

1   Click on the file named **Office Supplies** in the Faxes folder.

F2   2   Choose [File] Rename.

3   Change the name of the file to: **Brisbane Office Supplies** and press Enter.

4   In the Graphics folder, right click on the file named **hat**. Select Rename and change the file name to **Logo** then press Enter.

5   Click on the Graphics folder at the left of the window.

6   Rename the folder **Images**, in the same manner as you would rename a file.

Delete Files and Folders

Exercise 99

1   Right click on the file named **Logo** in the Images folder.

Delete   2   Select Delete. Click on Yes to delete the file and place it in the Recycle Bin.

3   Delete the Images folder.

Note You can select several files or folders (a group of folders can only be selected from the *right* of the window) and delete them all at one time.

Deleting a folder will also delete any files contained within that folder. You must ensure that you are deleting the correct files and folders before using this command.

Use the Right Mouse Button

The right mouse button may be used to quickly perform many common tasks in addition to those used in previous exercises.

Move/Copy Files

Exercise 100

1   Click on the Budget folder.

2   Select both files.

3   Move the mouse pointer over one of the selected files.

4   Click and drag with the *right* mouse button onto My Documents folder. When you release the mouse button a shortcut menu will appear.

5   Select Move Here. If you were copying files, you would select Copy Here.

Tip To copy files to a floppy disk in A: drive, right click on a selected file/s and choose Send To, 3½ Floppy (A).

Recycle Bin

Recycle Bin

* Scroll to the bottom of the folder list at the left of the Explorer window, and click on Recycle Bin OR double click on the Recycle Bin on your Desktop to display all deleted files.

* To restore files to their original folder, select them, right click and choose Restore OR choose [File] Restore.

* To delete files from the Recycle Bin, select and delete them in the usual manner. To delete *all* files, choose [File] Empty Recycle Bin. Files deleted from the Recycle Bin are gone forever!

Exercise 101

Create a folder structure for Care Cosmetics. The scenario you have worked with throughout the book will provide clues about folders and subfolders that would be used in this organisation, eg Staff, Sales Results.

Ensure that your structure is set up to create logical storage for all the Care Cosmetics files you have created so far, then move the files to your new filing system.

Exiting Windows Explorer

Exercise 102

➢   Choose [File] Close.

Manage Email Messages in Outlook

One of the main methods of receiving information in many organisations is by email. The range of information received by this medium is often more diverse than that received by any other means, and yet very often messages remain in a user's Inbox, in no logical order. Retrieval of old messages from an Inbox is often a time consuming guessing game, resulting in frustration and loss of important organisational information.

Organise Messages

Rules

It's a good idea to organise messages into different folders. In Outlook you can automatically direct emails that come from a certain person/company to a specific folder.

Exercise 103

1   Launch Outlook.

2   Click on Inbox on the Outlook Bar.

3   Click on the Organize button ⬚ on the Standard toolbar.

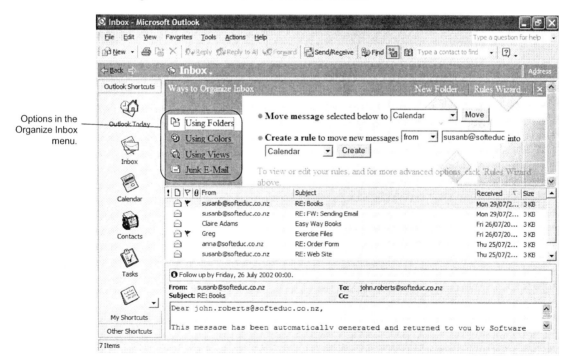

Options in the
Organize Inbox
menu.

In the *Ways to Organize Inbox* section you can select from a range of options – Using Folders, Using Colors, Using Views and Junk E-Mail.

Using Folders   New and old messages can be moved to certain folders automatically.

Using Colors   Email messages from different people/companies can be displayed in different colours, eg all emails from the boss are displayed in blue.

Using Views	Select the view you wish to use to list your email messages, eg by sender, conversation, topic, etc. This can also be done through [View] Current View.
Junk E-Mail	Unwanted spam and promotional email messages can be removed to a separate folder when received.

4   Click on the Organize button 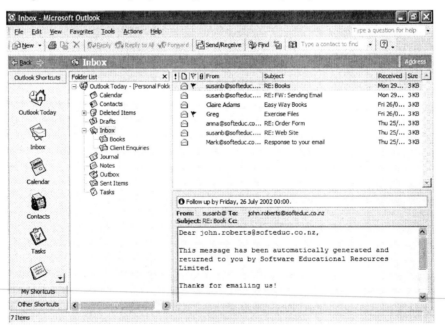 to turn off the display of Ways to Organize Inbox.

Folders

In the same way that a folder structure is created in Windows Explorer, new folders can also be created in Outlook to store different types of messages.

Exercise 104

Ctrl
Shift E

1   From the Inbox window choose [File] Folder, New Folder.

2   In the Name: box type: **Books**. Ensure the Folder contains: box displays Mail and Post Items.

3   In the Select where to place the folder: box click on 📁 Inbox . Click on OK.

4   Click on No, so that a shortcut is not added to the Outlook Bar.

The Books folder is displayed beneath Inbox in the Folder List. (Choose [View] Folder List if this is not displayed.) Additional folders can be added as shown in the example below, to store messages from different people or organisations, or by subject matter.

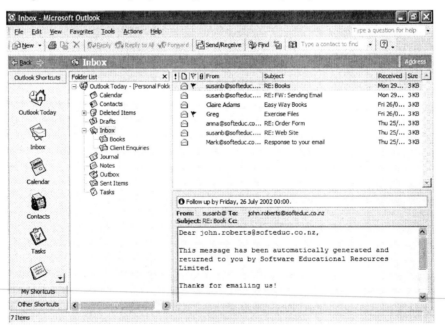

- Messages can be dragged from the Inbox and dropped in appropriate folders.

- If you wish to copy a message, hold down the Ctrl key while dragging.

- To move a selected message, click on the Move to Folder button 📁 and select the required folder.

- To delete a selected folder and its contents, press Delete, then click on Yes.

1   Create Outlook folders that would be suitable for managing email at Care Cosmetics.

2   Describe how you would use the *Ways to Organize Inbox* facility to further improve the efficiency of managing incoming email.

....

....

....

....

....

....

....

Store Paper-based Information

Filing Equipment

The choice of physical filing equipment within an office will depend upon several factors.

- Available space
- Volume and type of records
- Ease of use
- Accessibility requirements

Vertical Files

The vertical or "upright" filing system is most commonly used by businesses. Items are placed vertically, one behind the other in filing cabinets, drawers, or boxes.

Filing Cabinets (fixed)

The main advantage of using filing cabinets is that they are lockable and usually fireproof, as most are made of metal. Drawers can either be deep, to take large files, or shallow, to take cards or disks.

Most types of filing cabinet are used in conjunction with suspension files. These are suspended from metal rods and can be easily removed, rearranged or changed.

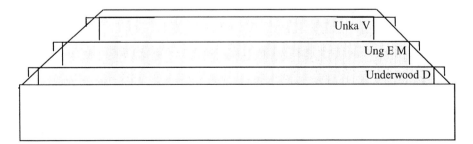

Filing Cabinets (mobile)

Mobile filing cabinets make maximum use of available space and can be made secure. They consist of back-to-back shelving systems on wheels that can be manoeuvred along metal tracks. Their versatility means that they are suitable for a variety of businesses. They can store large quantities of records and are often used in pharmacies where they act as storage for pharmaceutical items.

Card Indexes

Smaller vertical filing systems include small boxes or drawers that can be used to house index cards. These might be used for diary cards (one for each day) or customer details. File markers are used to indicate divisions and an identifying word, number or code is entered at the top of each card. Care must be taken to ensure that these types of files are locked away when not in use as they can be removed easily.

Storage for Large Documentation

Some businesses need to store very large items such as plans, maps or charts. Often these can be stored horizontally in specially designed drawers. It is also possible to purchase vertical suspension systems that use a series of hangers to hold documents.

Rotary Files

As the name suggests, rotary files rotate to provide access to documents. They are very useful in offices where space is at a premium.

Large files can be stored on circular filing shelves. These are rotated as required and this makes retrieval of information a quick and easy process. It also makes filing simpler because the person filing can just stand in one place and move the files. The disadvantage is that often these files cannot be stored securely. However, the system can be designed to suit the specific needs of the business and can be placed in a locked office if necessary.

Small rotary files can be used on desk tops. They provide easy access to information and require little space.

Rotary files can often be seen in doctors' surgeries and other places where there are large numbers of records and minimal available storage space.

Filing System Requirements

There are several important reasons for using a good filing system, which should provide safe and organised storage for records, as well as quick identification and retrieval. Filing might seem a menial, unimportant task, but it is a vital part of the business operation.

Certain filing system requirements are applicable to all businesses. They include:

- Ability to classify
- Ease of use
- Flexibility of organisation
- Preservation of information
- Long term practicality
- Time saving capabilities

Exercise 106

1 List three advantages of using an effective filing system.

   a ....

   b ....

   c ....

2 Name six requirements of a business filing system.

   a ....

   b ....

   c ....

   d ....

   e ....

   f ....

3 List three criteria that should be considered when choosing filing equipment.

   a ....

   b ....

   c ....

4 Describe a vertical filing system.

   ....

   ....

5 List two advantages of using filing cabinets.

   a ....

   b ....

6 What are suspension files?

   ....

   ....

7 What type of business might use mobile filing cabinets?

   ....

   ....

8 Small filing boxes can be very useful in a business situation. Name something that could be
   stored in them.

   ....

   ....

Classification Systems

Classification is a way of sorting items into separate sections so that they can be easily identified. When applied to filing, a classification system identifies files so that they can be organised in a logical manner.

Alphabetic

Arranging items alphabetically is the most common form of classification. The alphabetic system is easy to operate once established and it is widely recognised by most people. It is used by (for example) libraries and the producers of telephone directories, and also applies to dictionaries and encyclopaedias. Most businesses arrange their customer files in alphabetical order.

There are certain rules that should be followed. Surprisingly, it is not as simple as following the alphabet from A - Z. Last name variations such as Mc and Mac can become very confusing unless they are placed in the correct order.

If a business decides to use an alphabetical filing system, they first have to decide on names they will use to identify files. Customers are normally classified according to their last names, with their first names or initials following. There are certain rules that can be followed to ensure that alphabetically stored files are always located in the correct place.

File by last name.

Underwood D
Ung EM
Unka V

Where last names are the same, file in order of initials or first names.

Smith K G
Smith Lester
Smith LW

Notice that "Smith LW" has been placed after "Smith Lester". This is because the classification uses a combination of full names and initials. If "Smith LW" was "Smith Larry W", then this file would be placed before "Smith Lester".

The same rules apply to the names of organisations.

Thomson J
Thomson & King Surveyors
Thomson K & JG

The '&' between the two names is ignored. That is why "King", beginning with Ki is listed before K & JG (taken as being K followed by J).

The prefix "Mc" is treated as "Mac" and the next letter in the name determines the position in the filing system.

MacAlister R
McAllister P
McHugh L

This is one of the most poorly enforced rules.

Where a business name includes initials, the initials determine the filing order.

PL Shoe Store
Pugh A T
PWJ Enterprises

The prefix "St" should be sorted as "Saint". The next letter in the name determines filing order.

Sainsbury P D
St George W
St John Ambulance
Sinton Shoes

Hyphenated and compound names must be sorted according to the first part, with the next letter determining filing order.

Vallance K
Van Eyk R
Vaughan-Williams D

Titles (if used) should be placed at the end of the name.

Evans A   Mr
Evans E   Dr
Evans L   Mrs

When numbers are used at the beginning of the name, they should be filed in order of the spelling of the number when it is expressed as a word.

54 The Club   (Fifty)
321 Taxi Service   (Three)
24 Hour Service Station   (Twenty)

This may sound a little complicated and very unlike the simple alphabetical order with which we are most familiar; however, once the rules have been established and followed, it then becomes a straightforward classification system.

Numeric

When there is a large volume of records to be filed, numbers rather than names may be used. A numeric filing system can be extremely versatile. In addition, this type of classification offers greater security than that provided by an alphabetic system, as security codes can be incorporated.

One of the problems with a numbering system, however, is that if all customers are organised numerically, the number of a particular customer has to be known before the file can be located. This may involve extra work. However, this should not become a problem if the organisation has developed or adapted their filing system accordingly. Libraries are organisations that successfully use both numeric and alphabetic filing systems; they cross reference the two. Books can be found by authors or by serial numbers.

There are various methods that can be used in a numeric system. These include:

Straight numbering

This is the easiest of all filing systems. All you have to do is to file according to number order, starting with the digit at the left.

61159000
61160000
61161000

Care has to be taken with filing if the numbers are long because it is easy to misplace a file and can be very difficult to locate it.

Middle digit numbering

If there are many files and classifications, the numbers can be coded, with each section representing a piece of information. Middle digit numbering involves the use of three sets of digits, usually with two numbers in each. Each set represents something different. In the following example the middle set indicates the location of the file (eg drawer number). The first set shows the area of the filing system (folder or section) and the last set shows the file number/order within that system.

12 -**15** - 54   (Drawer **15**, Section 12, File 54)
12 -**15** - 55
13 -**15** - 23

Therefore, all the files above can be found in drawer 15. The first two are in section 12 and the last one in section 13. The file number refers to the order in which items will be filed.

Terminal digit numbering

Terminal digit filing is very similar to the middle digit system. The main difference is that the number is read backwards in twos.

10 - 18 - **21**   (Drawer **21**, Section 18, File 10)
10 - 19 - **21**
10 - 20 - **21**

Therefore, the first set of digits shown above would be read in the order 21- 18 - 10. In this case, the drawer number is 21, the section number is 18 and the file number of the item is 10.

There are many other methods of numeric filing. Some include a combination of numbers and letters. For example, 30/11/46 SW could relate to a numeric filing system located in the office of Sally Wilkinson. Organisations tend to customise their filing systems to meet their own requirements.

In a numeric filing system, a register of numbers is kept in order to identify customers, etc. Many businesses allocate customer numbers from such a register.

Client Register – Care Cosmetics

Number	Name
1092349	Arnold Healthfoods
1092350	Atkinson Cosmetics
1092351	Azure Enterprises (Mary Fenwick)
1092352	
1092353	
1092354	
1092355	Baker Skincare Consultants
1092356	Banfield Beauty Therapists
1092357	
1092358	
1092359	
1092360	

Exercise 107

1   Arrange the following names into alphabetic order using the established alphabetic filing system.

Dilks K & F	1 ....
Darrow LM	2 ....
Darroch GM	3 ....
Darrow LW & P	4 ....
Davis SH	5 ....
Davies Ida	6 ....
David Carey Plumbers	7 ....

2   Now arrange the following into alphabetic order.

McInerney BS	1 ....
MacDonald Y	2 ....
McDonald PJ	3 ....
McGee R	4 ....
McGiven Electricians	5 ....
Mace T	6 ....
McCarty Peter	7 ....

3   Sort the following 'Saints' into order.

St Francis Xavier School   1 ....
Saint Y & F   2 ....
St Johns Church Hall   3 ....
St Johns Community Club   4 ....
Saint-John Victor   5 ....
St James Church   6 ....
Saint C & H   7 ....

4   Try sorting a few numbers this time!

777 The Terrace Club   1 ....
24 Hour Pharmacy   2 ....
509 Brighton Line   3 ....
101 Dalmations   4 ....
904 Hair Design   5 ....
66 Cafe   6 ....
321 Disco Fun   7 ....

5   Use the middle digit numbering system to sort the following into order.

19 - 27 - 98   1 ....
19 - 27 - 92   2 ....
19 - 27 - 87   3 ....
19 - 26 - 51   4 ....
19 - 26 - 75   5 ....
19 - 27 - 95   6 ....
19 - 26 - 53   7 ....

6   Use the terminal digit numbering system for the following.

34 - 80 - 67   1 ....
34 - 75 - 41   2 ....
34 - 80 - 66   3 ....
34 - 80 - 61   4 ....
34 - 75 - 49   5 ....
34 - 75 - 44   6 ....
34 - 80 - 65   7 ....

Prepare Documents for Filing

Is it ready to be filed?

Care must be taken to ensure that documents to be filed have been released for filing. In a large office, new documents are not usually removed for filing until they have been allocated a release mark, or authorisation to file. This can be initialled by the person who has finished with the document. Exceptions to this rule could be copies of letters sent out of the office and any related incoming correspondence (which should be attached).

The procedure in smaller offices may be slightly different, but it is still necessary to receive verbal confirmation that a document can be filed.

What should be checked on the actual document?

1   Remove staples and paper clips if not required. Paper clips can easily become dislodged or catch onto other papers within a file, so it is preferable to use staples.

2   If a document is torn, repair it with transparent tape.

3   Check to see if there are related documents and put them together, ready to be filed.

4   If a document is very small and could get lost, it should be taped onto a larger piece of paper. Alternatively, it could be placed in a marked envelope or plastic holder.

Should it be placed in a new folder before filing?

If the document relates to a new customer, it may be necessary to prepare a new folder. This should be created according to the filing system in use.

Does it require indexing/coding?

In a library filing system, books are indexed according to their categories (fiction, non-fiction, hobbies, etc) and they are coded according to their position within the library. These codes are usually placed on the spine of the books.

Office filing systems are similar. A code is usually written in the top right corner of every file. Alternatively, where a filing system uses customer names an additional coding number might not be required.

Does the document require cross-referencing?

Cross-referencing links up related documents in a filing system. Sometimes it might be necessary to photocopy a document in order to store it in two separate locations. In this case, coding and indexing relates to both locations.

Entire files can be cross referenced. For example, a lawyer may have a file for a client who conducts business transactions under her maiden name and private transactions in her married name. She could have two separate files that are cross referenced.

Jenkins Sally	1059
See Harrison Sally	

Harrison Sally	1032
See Jenkins Sally	

Sort Documentation

Sorting documents before filing begins will save time. In addition, it gives another opportunity to check that each document is ready for filing. If there are many documents, portable sorting trays with dividers, or separate baskets, may be used.

Exercise 108

1   Note three points that should be checked on a paper-based record before it is filed.

   a ....

   b ....

   c ....

2   Describe an example of an occasion when you would have to prepare a new folder before manually filing a document.

   ....

   ....

3   Define the following filing terms.

   Indexing:

   ....

   ....

   Coding:

   ....

   ....

   Cross referencing:

   ....

   ....

File Sharing

Great care must be taken when moving files and documentation because they can be mislaid, and cause inconvenience.

The best way to avoid losing files is to keep a record of when they are moved and who is in possession of them. This is essential in large businesses to track files that will move, not only between people, but between departments in different locations.

Tracking methods include:

File Markers

These can be left in the place of the file to indicate who has borrowed it and when it was taken. Markers need to be durable and easily seen. This system works well in a business where movement of files is minimal.

Cards

Instead of markers, cards can be used to identify who has taken a file and when. The cards fit into the spaces left by absent files.

Single Entry Movement Cards

These are placed inside pockets within files. As with other methods, the card records details of who has borrowed a file, and when it is removed. Every time a file is borrowed, the card is removed and stored in a customised box or container. When a file is returned, the card is replaced. This is the system used by some libraries when issuing books. In larger libraries, books are issued electronically through a computer system that records all the necessary information.

Arnold Health foods			2075643
Location	*Date*	*Location*	*Date*

Exercise 109

Describe in your own words two methods that can be used to ensure efficient movement and monitoring of files around an office.

1 ....

....

....

....

....

....

....

2 ....

....

....

....

....

....

Exercise 110

Staff records at Care Cosmetics are paper based. Discuss appropriate options and solutions for a staff record filing system.

Equipment:

....
....
....
....
....
....
....
....

Classification system:

....
....
....
....
....
....
....
....

Procedures for filing, accessing and removing records:

....
....
....
....
....
....
....
....

Section

5

Review Information Needs

Learning Outcomes

At the end of this section you should be able to -

❑   Obtain feedback to ensure relevancy, accuracy and sufficiency of information.

❑   Use feedback to ensure that information collected is suitable for analysis, decision-making and the development of plans, strategies and options.

❑   Review contribution of information to decision-making and modify collection methods as necessary.

❑   Identify future information needs and incorporate into modified collection methods.

❑   Document future information needs and incorporate into modified reporting processes.

Introduction

In sections 1 to 4 a number of methods of collecting, assessing, organising and presenting information were considered. Whatever methods are used, they should never represent the end of the information management process. The final and most critical steps are to establish whether or not the information is meeting the needs of its users, and if not, to make the modifications needed.

Feedback Methods

One of the most important tools to use in reviewing the effectiveness of information is to ask the users of it for their comments. Users of information could be external, such as clients or suppliers of an organisation, or could be internal, as is the case in the Care Cosmetics scenario.

Methods of obtaining feedback include:

- Verbal questioning
- Focus groups
- Written surveys/questionnaires
- Suggestion boxes
- Noting complaints made

Verbal Questioning

Many people won't feel comfortable offering any criticism in a one-to-one or face-to-face situation. This can result in feedback that is not particularly helpful, as unidentified problems may remain a barrier to the ongoing effectiveness of the information.

Focus Groups

Feedback obtained in this way can be very balanced, and may also result in useful suggestions for improvements. Large organisations will often form customer focus groups to consider issues such as the brand name of a product, for example.

One distinct advantage of obtaining feedback in this way is in the interaction of the information users with each other. The "brainstorming" that tends to occur in these situations can result in truly innovative and productive ideas.

How to Run a Focus Group

The purpose of a focus group is to target a specific area or question with a group of people who are closely affected by the area or question.

Tightly define what your focus group will discuss

Don't have too wide a remit for your focus group. For example, if you work for a publishing house and publish travel books, children's books and books for accountants, don't attempt to have a single focus group which covers all your books. At best, the accountants won't have a view on your children's book range, and at worst they will become very bored and 'switch off' from your meeting.

Who to invite

It is important to include a broad range of individuals where possible so that you get a good cross-section of viewpoints. Don't avoid including those who have been critical of the organisation or service provided – these people are the ones who can provide the most help when it comes to making improvements.

Agenda

To get the most out of the focus group, prepare an agenda before the meeting and circulate it to the participants. Ask if there is anything they would like added to the agenda (this makes people feel involved and gives you some prior notice of topics that may arise). Make sure you leave plenty of time at the end of the meeting for "any other business", ie other issues that participants want to raise.

Encourage participants to talk to each other

Perhaps have a coffee session before the meeting starts, to break the ice. Ensure that everyone knows who everyone else is.

Remember that you are there to learn

Your focus group is being held so that YOU can gain information from it. To do this effectively participants must feel that they are being listened to – otherwise they will clam up and be reluctant to speak. Therefore, it is important to give people a chance to speak critically as well as positively. Take notes on all comments presented; you can determine the validity of the information after the meeting.

Follow-up

Ensure participants know that what they have told you is valued – make sure that they are thanked and kept informed of what changes occur as a result of your meeting. In many cases it is appropriate to provide a small token of thanks, particularly where customers have been involved. (A voucher for your service or products may be appropriate.)

Exercise 111

Briefly describe the steps you would take to establish and run a focus group of Care Cosmetics' branch managers to evaluate the collection of information from branches, and the usefulness of the summarised company information that is returned to branches. Make a list of agenda items.

....

....

....

....

....

....

....

....

....

....

....

....

....

Written Surveys

Written questionnaires are commonly used in service industries such as hotels, restaurants and training centres. The expectation is that the client will complete a questionnaire after they have received a service (ie hospitality, meal, or training course).

Another popular use of questionnaires is to conduct surveys within an organisation. These may cover any of a wide range of issues and are particularly useful where a large number of people need to be surveyed, or where careful thought needs to be applied by the respondents (written answers tend to facilitate this better than verbal answers).

Examples of the use of written surveys in organisation are:

- Staff satisfaction surveys – used to assess, amend and implement new policy/procedures in an organisation.

- Upward performance appraisals – questions completed by subordinates relating to the perceived effectiveness of their manager, used to form part of the manager's overall performance review.

When considering the above examples it becomes obvious that confidentiality and anonymity are often key issues when questionnaires are used internally in an organisation.

The main issues to consider when using questionnaires are:

- The wording of questions must be easily understood and must provide the opportunity to collect relevant feedback. For example, the question "Did you enjoy your meal?" is completely inadequate unless the question "Why?" is added.

- The questionnaire cannot be too lengthy or respondents will tend to lose interest and either not answer, or worse, not consider their answers carefully. A maximum of three to four carefully worded questions is ideal.

- Questionnaires should usually be anonymous. The opportunity can be provided for respondents to identify themselves if they wish, and/or to be contacted; this can be particularly useful in the case of customer satisfaction surveys, where previously unheard customer complaints may be presented and an opportunity to resolve them provided. Where surveys are used internally within an organisation, anonymity is usually extremely important if truthful and useful feedback is to be obtained, as previously discussed.

- Try to have customer satisfaction questionnaires completed as soon as possible after the service has been provided, otherwise people tend to forget what their impression was at the time, and/or lose interest in completing and returning the survey.

- Finally, the completed questionnaires need to be reviewed – there is no point in having them completed if they're not going to be read!

Exercise 112

Use Word to create two questionnaires – one to be completed by branch managers, and the second by senior management – to evaluate the effectiveness of the Care Cosmetics sales spreadsheet and PowerPoint presentation and to encourage ideas for improvements. Comment on the degree of importance of anonymity in the case of each management group.

Resources to help you:

- *Care Cosmetics scenario (beginning of the book)*
- *Questioning Techniques, pages 21 to 23*
- *Written Surveys, above*

Suggestion Boxes

There are many parallels between suggestion boxes and written surveys. Suggestion boxes provide a more open forum for respondents to comment on anything they see fit, at any time. It is important, if this system is used, that it is openly seen to be effective. This happens when it is obvious that the suggestion box is cleared regularly, when public acknowledgements of suggestions are made. An example of this could be a sign temporarily placed on a customer service desk –

> *As a result of a suggestion from one of our customers, we now have fridge magnets printed with the name and direct line of your personal customer service representative. Please ask for your free magnet today.*

Complaints Handling

Ideally, if the correct processes are followed to manage information effectively, complaints should be few and far between. If they do occur, however, they can certainly provide useful feedback. When considering complaints, it is always useful to look beyond the obvious. For example, a complaint that "the sales results presented at meetings aren't clear", could mean that:

- Visual presentations contain too much information, or are too detailed;

- The lighting or arrangement of furniture in the meeting room needs to be reconsidered;

- The presenter needs to revise his/her explanations or speak more audibly;

- The results are presented in a manner that is boring and fails to retain the attention of the audience.

Audits

A combination of several of the above feedback methods could be combined into a branch visit, or audit. While the term "audit" conjures pictures of a very one-sided meeting, a well-executed audit can easily become a meeting that combines the formal requirements of an audit with the communication principles of feedback. This, in effect, creates a useful two-way feedback process. The advantage of this style of feedback is that areas are covered consistently (as is required in an audit situation), and all areas important to the organisation are covered, not just those deemed important by the parties providing the feedback. An example of this process in action is outlined later in this topic.

Preparing well for an audit is even more essential than the actual audit itself! Usual procedures for a standard audit in the form of a visit would be as follows.

1   Determine what is required from the audit.

   Example: Is sales information being collected accurately and efficiently in branches, and is the collated sales information for the company being used correctly in branches?

2   Make a check list of items to be covered during the audit – be precise.

Example:

☐   Sales stats collection sheet being used by every staff member

☐   Sample of collection sheets checked for accuracy

☐   Sales meeting observed – information disseminated to staff effectively

☐   Sales information on staff room notice board

    etc...

3   Communicate details of the audit to those directly involved. Include as much advance warning as possible, and provide as much information as possible.

4   Complete the audit, adhering strictly to the prepared checklist and using the same format for all audits (assuming there is more than one to be completed).

5   Allow time to elicit feedback from those involved in the audit – the process of the audit frequently uncovers areas that are not on the check list, but are nevertheless relevant and important to address.

Example: Sales information is in an untidy heap on the staffroom table, instead of displayed on a notice board as required. Feedback on this determines that the branch manager has "run out" of stationery budget, and so has not purchased a notice board for the staff room. This may lead to further discussion surrounding issues of the branch manager's financial management skills, or may even uncover instances of fraud or theft. (Where is the original notice board issued to the branch? What has the entire stationery budget been spent on so early in the year?)

Exercise 113

The following scenario outlines the results of feedback obtained during an audit of branches to assess the management of sales information at Care Cosmetics. Use Word to create an audit check list that would result in the findings outlined below.

The following issues that compromised the integrity of sales information were discovered during an audit of all four Care Cosmetics branches and Head Office.

1   Managers were transferred between branches during the last six months. This has resulted in confusion regarding what sales information was collected at each branch, as each manager had different ideas about what was required.

2   Some managers are "reinventing the wheel". At Brisbane branch, the manager is an extremely competent Excel user. The type of information he collects from his branch, and the way in which he presents it, are both valid, but don't conform to the system that has been put in place.

3   In some cases, the incorrect information is being collected from the trial balance, resulting in inaccurate sales results being submitted.

4   At Head Office level, data entry errors are occurring when information received from branches is loaded into the sales results spreadsheet.

5   Collated information is not getting to branch managers quickly enough from Head Office. Managers need an immediate focus on sales results in order to motivate their staff and achieve their budgets. Finding out what other branches achieved half way through the following month is almost useless.

6   Some branches are not meeting organisational requirements in terms of confidentiality, with sales results being posted in clear view of all clients.

When you have completed the audit check list, check your answers with the solution on page 177.

Read the Care Cosmetics scenario at the beginning of the book. What additional information security issue exists which is not mentioned in the notes from the branch audit? Describe the nature of the risk.

....

....

....

....

Understand the Nature of Feedback

Constructive Feedback

Nobody produces work that is absolutely perfect. Everybody has room to improve. The most successful people are those who have realised that they will never stop learning, however old or expert they become.

As it applies to managing information in an organisation, constructive feedback consists of a balanced and focused view of a process – ie does the information do the job for which it was intended?

Quality feedback will typically address any of the following points.

- What is working well
- What isn't working well
- Ideas for improvement

Valid Feedback

Not all feedback is valid. Providing constructive feedback is a learned skill that not all individuals possess. Valid feedback is:

- focused on the issue;
- factual;
- neither unnecessarily critical, nor unnecessarily favourable;
- stated in professional terms, rather than on a personal level.

This is not to say that you need necessarily agree with feedback in order for it to be valid. The reason for you to assess whether or not feedback is valid is only to enable you to avoid being distracted by that which is invalid.

How to Encourage Feedback

1 Most people will only provide feedback if you ask for it, so make a practice of asking.

2 When you receive verbal feedback, use positive body language. It can be difficult to give honest feedback verbally, and the task is made easier if the recipient is receptive.

3 Show your appreciation for the time and effort given in providing feedback. In the case of customer feedback, it may sometimes be appropriate to provide a small gift as a token of thanks, as previously mentioned.

4 Act on feedback given where appropriate. When others can see positive changes occurring as a result of feedback they have provided, it encourages them to keep offering it.

Exercise 115

You have just delivered a PowerPoint presentation to a Care Cosmetics management meeting. Feedback from your presentation is as follows. Indicate which statements are valid and which are invalid, and state your reasons.

Statement	Valid	Invalid

Statement   Valid   Invalid

The presentation was a bit too long (45 minutes).   ☐   ☐

Reason ....

....

Statement   Valid   Invalid

The presenter's suit was far too bright and her voice very grating.   ☐   ☐

Reason ....

....

Statement   Valid   Invalid

I thought the afternoon tea was absolutely wonderful – definitely the best
sausage rolls I've had in a long time. The presentation was really fantastic – the
PowerPoint presentation had really great colours and pictures in it and I thought   ☐   ☐
the presenter could easily have been a professional television newsreader, as her
overall pronunciation and personal presentation were of such a high standard.

Reason ....

....

Statement   Valid   Invalid

The charts shown didn't clearly depict the information in a relevant way – most
unusual to display the trend of growing sales over the past year as a pie chart.   ☐   ☐

Reason ....

....

Statement   Valid   Invalid

The presenter is too short – get a taller one.   ☐   ☐

Reason ....

....

Statement   Valid   Invalid

It was difficult to see the presenter – a lectern would have solved this problem.   ☐   ☐

Reason ....

....

Evaluate Feedback

An evaluation form can be a useful tool to summarise feedback so that the "big picture" may be seen. As discussed, not all feedback collected will be relevant or valid, and an evaluation form can help to discard such feedback and retain that which focuses on the issue.

In Section 2, two spreadsheets were developed to meet specific information needs for Care Cosmetics. Shown below is an example of an evaluation form that has been used to evaluate the Care Cosmetics mobile phone spreadsheet on page 91.

Spreadsheet Evaluation Form

General Questions

	Yes	No
Does the spreadsheet solve the problem?	☑	☐
Is the formatting appropriate for the data and type of problem?	☑	☐
Can you read and clearly understand the spreadsheet?	☑	☐
Is the spreadsheet presented attractively?	☑	☐
The data and calculations within the spreadsheet are accurate?	☑	☐

Modifications

Format all amounts to dollars $

	Yes	No
After modifications have been made to the spreadsheet, does it solve the problem?	☑	☐

Exercise 116

View the spreadsheet you created on pages 93 to 95. Use the form below to evaluate its effectiveness.

Spreadsheet Evaluation Form

General Questions

	Yes	No
Does the spreadsheet solve the problem?	☐	☐
Is the formatting appropriate for the data and type of problem?	☐	☐
Can you read and clearly understand the spreadsheet?	☐	☐
Is the spreadsheet presented attractively?	☐	☐
The data and calculations within the spreadsheet are accurate?	☐	☐

Modifications

_____

_____

_____

_____

_____

_____

_____

_____

_____

_____

	Yes	No
After modifications have been made to the spreadsheet, does it solve the problem?	☐	☐

Exercise 117

Open the presentation called **Cruise Holidays**. The presentation is about cruises for a target audience of adults with extra spending money. It is designed to convey holidaying in luxury on a cruise ship and the details of the cruises including costs.

View the presentation in Normal View and Slide Show View, then answer the questions in the evaluation form below.

PowerPoint Presentation Evaluation Form

Presentation Topic: ....

Purpose of presentation: ....

Target Audience: ....

Date of Presentation: ....

Estimated Length of Presentation (time): ....

Rate the presentation, in relation to effective communication:

	Fair	Good	Very Good	Excellent
Order of presentation of information	☐	☐	☐	☐
Attractiveness	☐	☐	☐	☐
Readability	☐	☐	☐	☐
Appropriateness for target audience	☐	☐	☐	☐

	Yes	No
Does the content of the presentation meet the purpose for which it was intended?	☐	☐
Does the content meet the target audience?	☐	☐

Open the PowerPoint presentation you created in Section 3 on pages 112 to 116. Use the form below to evaluate the presentation in terms of its effectiveness.

PowerPoint Presentation Evaluation Form

Presentation Topic: ....

Purpose of presentation: ....

Target Audience: ....

Date of Presentation: ....

Estimated Length of Presentation (time): ....

Rate the presentation, in relation to effective communication:

	Fair	Good	Very Good	Excellent
Order of presentation of information	☐	☐	☐	☐
Attractiveness	☐	☐	☐	☐
Readability	☐	☐	☐	☐
Appropriateness for target audience	☐	☐	☐	☐

	Yes	No
Does the content of the presentation meet the purpose for which it was intended?	☐	☐
Does the content meet the target audience?	☐	☐

What Modifications are Needed?

Exercise 119

The issues identified during the Care Cosmetics branch audit (page 164) are re-stated below. For each issue, note an appropriate solution.

1   Managers were transferred between branches during the last six months. This has resulted in confusion regarding what sales information was collected at each branch, as each manager had different ideas about what was required.

....

....

2   Some managers are "reinventing the wheel". At Brisbane branch, the manager is an extremely competent Excel user. The type of information he collects from his branch, and the way in which he presents it, are both valid, but don't conform to the system that has been put in place.

....

....

3   In some cases, the incorrect information is being collected from the trial balance, resulting in inaccurate sales results being submitted.

....

....

....

4   At Head Office level, data entry errors are occurring when information received from branches is loaded into the sales results spreadsheet.

....

....

....

5   Collated information is not getting to branch managers quickly enough from Head Office. Managers need an immediate focus on sales results in order to motivate their staff and achieve their budgets. Finding out what other branches achieved half way through the following month is almost useless.

....

....

....

6   Some branches are not meeting organisational requirements in terms of confidentiality, with sales results being posted in clear view of all clients.

....

....

....

Compare your answers with the suggested solutions on page 177. Remember, there may well be more than one appropriate solution in each case – do not assume your answers are wrong simply because they differ from the suggested solutions.

Modify Systems

Several areas have been identified where modifications must be made to improve the usefulness of sales information for Care Cosmetics. In the following exercise you will address issues 4 and 5 (see page 178) by producing a spreadsheet that can be prepared at branch level, and quickly and accurately collated at Head Office to produce company results.

Exercise 120

1   Open Excel, and the **Care Cosmetics Sales** workbook.

2   Right click on the November Sales worksheet tab and select Move or Copy

3   Click on the To book: ▼ and select (new book).

4   Click in the *Create a copy* check box then click on OK.

5   Save the new workbook with the name **Sydney Branch Sales**

6   Delete the pie chart.

7   Change the name of the November Sales worksheet to **Sydney Sales Results**

8   Create three more copies of the Sydney Sales Results worksheet, leaving them in the Sydney Branch workbook.

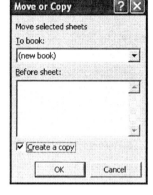

Modify Multiple Worksheets

Where the same changes are required to several worksheets, the entire group of sheets should be selected; the changes made in one will then reflect in every worksheet in the selected group.

Exercise 121

1   With the first worksheet tab selected, hold Shift and use the worksheet navigation buttons to move to the last worksheet tab. Click on the last tab to select all four sheets.

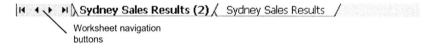

Worksheet navigation buttons

2   Click in row header 7 and drag down to select rows 7 to 11.

3   Right click on the selection and choose Delete.

4   Delete the contents of cells B6 to E6.

5   Click in column header F to select the column.

6   Right click and choose Insert.

7   In cell F4, type the heading: **Total** and press Enter.

8   Click in cell A6, type: **xx** and press Enter.

9   Use the =SUM function in cell F6 to add the contents of cells B6 to E6.

10   Edit the heading in cell A1 to read: **Care Cosmetics xx Branch**

11   Change the contents of cell A2 to: **Month:**

Add a Footer

The spreadsheet that has been created is intended to become a standard part of Care Cosmetics' organisational documentation, so it should conform to any existing standards. In order to achieve this, the company logo and a footer containing relevant company information will be added. The footer may be added at this point, and will apply to all selected worksheets. It is not possible to add a logo to several worksheets at once, so this will occur individually after the worksheets have been deselected.

1   With the group of worksheets selected, choose [View] Header and Footer.

2   Click on the Custom Footer button in the Header/Footer tab.

3   With the cursor located in the Left section: box, type: **Care Cosmetics**

4   Select the text and click on the Font button **A**.

5   Change the font to Arial 8 pt and click on OK.

6   In the Center section: box, add the text – **Confidential** – and change the font to Arial 8 pt.

7   In the Right section: box click on the Date button ▦ to add a field that will always reflect the current date. Change the font of the field to Arial 8 pt.

8   Click on OK, then on OK again.

9   Click on the Print Preview button ▱ then on the footer to view it. Click on the footer again, then click on the Close button to return to Normal view.

10   Click on the Sydney Sales Results sheet tab to ungroup the worksheets.

Add a Logo

1   Click in cell G1 in the Sydney Sales Results worksheet.

2   Choose [Insert] Picture, From File.

3   Locate and double click on the file named **Care Cosmetics Logo** in My Documents folder to add it to the worksheet.

4   Click on the image and hold Alt (to retain the proportions of the image) as you drag on the re-size handles to fit the logo over cells G1 to G3.

	A	B	C	D	E	F	G
1	Care Cosmetics xx Branch						
2	Month:						RE COSMETICS
3							
4		Week 1	Week 2	Week 3	Week 4	Total	Average Sales
5							
6	xx					0	#DIV/0!

5   Preview the worksheet, then return to Normal view.

Replace Variable Text

The use of placeholder text (xx) allows variable information in the worksheets (ie branch names) to be entered efficiently, using the Find and Replace function.

Ctrl H   1   Choose [Edit] Replace.

2   Type: **xx** in the Find what: box and **Sydney** in the Replace with: box

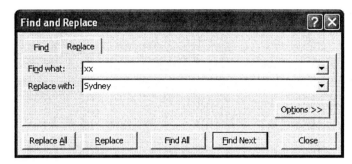

3   Click on Replace All then click on OK and Close.

4   Rename the Sydney Sales Results (2) worksheet **Melbourne Sales Results**

5   Use the Find and Replace function to replace xx with **Melbourne**

6   Add the Care Cosmetics logo to the worksheet in the same manner as for the Sydney Sales Results worksheet.

7   Modify the remaining two worksheets in the same manner for Brisbane and Perth branches, changing the worksheet names, replacing the variable text, and adding the logo.

8   Right click on the Melbourne Sales Results worksheet tab.

9   Select Move or Copy.

10 Move the worksheet to a new workbook and save with the name **Melbourne Branch Sales**

11 Return to the **Sydney Branch Sales** workbook. Move the Brisbane and Perth worksheets into separate workbooks and save each in the same manner.

Protect Worksheets

When worksheets are distributed to users who may not be very familiar with Excel, it is wise to prevent them from being changed, except where necessary. In this case, the only cells that need to be changed by branch staff are the actual sales figures for weeks 1 to 4.

1   In the Sydney Branch Sales workbook, select cells B6 to E6.

2   Choose [Format] Cells and click on the Protection tab.

3   Click in the *Locked* option check box to remove the tick, and click on OK.

Cells are only locked when a worksheet is protected, so the next steps are essential to controlling access to worksheet cells.

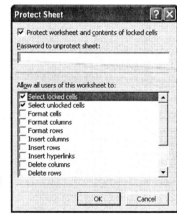

4   Choose [Tools] Protection, Protect Sheet.

In this case, a password will not be applied (although this option can provide extra security where required).

The access options to be made available may be chosen from the Allow all users of this worksheet to: box. In this case, ensure the two options shown at the right are selected.

5   Click on OK and save the changes to the workbook.

You can test the protection by attempting to enter data into both locked and unlocked cells – ensure you delete the results of your experimentation!

6   Protect and save the remaining three branch workbooks.

Exercise 122

Individual files have now been prepared for each branch to use to record sales results. In Section 2 (pages 96 to 97) the importance of documenting the use of spreadsheets was discussed, an example provided, and the version of the sales spreadsheet used at Head Office was documented.

1　Create a new worksheet in the Sydney Branch Sales workbook, and name the new worksheet: **Instructions**

2　Use the worksheet to document basic instructions for branch staff to use the spreadsheet. The following example illustrates the expected appearance of the spreadsheet when it is returned from a branch (this should assist you in developing documentation).

	A	B	C	D	E	F	G
1	**Care Cosmetics Sydney Branch**						
2	**Month:**						
3							
4		*Week 1*	*Week 2*	*Week 3*	*Week 4*	*Total*	*Average Sales*
5							
6	Sydney	4,320	4,441	7,980	6,650	23,391	5,848

3　Copy the completed Instructions worksheet into each branch sales workbook, then save and close all workbooks, including **Care Cosmetics Sales**. (Hold Shift and choose [File], Close All, saving changes if prompted to do so.)

Exercise 123

1　Launch Outlook.

2　Draft an example email message to a branch manager of your choice, explaining the revisions that have been made to the sales collection information process. Ensure you attach the spreadsheet file for the relevant branch to your message.

3　Print the message, then send to a classmate's email address OR close without sending.

Collate Spreadsheet Data

The final step in the modification process is to collate and distribute the sales information using the new system. In the following exercise sales information has been received from all branches for the month of December and is ready to be copied into the sales spreadsheet for the entire organisation.

Exercise 124

1　Open the following files. (Hold Ctrl to select all four files from the Open dialog box, then click on Open)

Sydney Branch Sales – Dec　　　　**Brisbane Branch Sales – Dec**
Melbourne Branch Sales – Dec　　**Perth Branch Sales – Dec**

2　Open the **Care Cosmetics Sales** workbook and save it as **Care Cosmetics Sales – Dec**

3　Erase the November data – remember to leave the formulas in place.

4　Change all references to the month of November in the worksheet, to **December**

5　Copy and paste the December data from each branch workbook into the relevant row of the **Care Cosmetics Sales – Dec** workbook.

> **Note** As both charts are linked to the spreadsheet data, they will be automatically updated.

6　Save and print the workbook using the [File] Print command and choosing the *Entire workbook* option. Close Excel and all workbooks.

Consider Future Information Needs

The modifications made to improve the processing of sales information for Care Cosmetics were extremely simple. It would have been possible to create a far more automated spreadsheet solution, but in this case it was inappropriate in view of the likely future information needs of Care Cosmetics.

- With rapid growth, and more branches expected to be opened in the short term, it is important to have systems in place that are simple enough to be flexible. The type of information needed is likely to grow and change as quickly as the organisation does, so putting complex systems in place at this point that will very likely need to be changed several times in the foreseeable future, is an inefficient exercise.

- New branches mean new staff, and it is likely that many will not be particularly competent Excel users, so spreadsheet solutions need to be kept simple in order for branch staff to be able to use them easily.

- The accounting system upgrade that is proposed over the next year will mean that the entire Care Cosmetics operation is incorporated into one entity for reporting purposes. At that point, it should be possible for the sales information to be downloaded for each branch and the entire organisation on a daily basis, via the trial balance. This will eliminate the need for the collection of this particular type of information manually from branches, so again, it is not an effective use of resources to excessively develop the manual collection system at this point.

Exercise 125

Review the Care Cosmetics scenario at the beginning of the book. Consider the developments that have occurred throughout the book. What other information management systems do you foresee a requirement for at Care Cosmetics in the future?

....
....
....
....
....
....
....
....
....
....
....
....
....
....

Solutions

Exercise 113 – Audit check list

☐ Sales information collected is complete and accurate – verify against trial balance.

☐ Information collection system has been implemented in branch.

☐ Information collated accurately from branch results – check branch handwritten information submitted against spreadsheet produced at head office.

☐ Timelines are being adhered to for submission of information from branches to head office, and collated information from head office to branches.

☐ Sales information is being displayed appropriately on staffroom notice board.

Exercise 119 – Suggested solutions to issues discovered during audit

1 Managers were transferred between branches during the last six months. This has resulted in confusion regarding what sales information was collected at each branch, as each manager had different ideas about what was required.

Solution: A standard, documented system which operates across every branch will resolve this issue; the information collection process will not require input from the branch manager, other than in a monitoring role to ensure it is completed in accordance with organisational requirements.

2 Some managers are "reinventing the wheel". At Brisbane branch, the manager is an extremely competent Excel user. The type of information he collects from his branch, and the way in which he presents it, are both valid, but don't conform to the system that has been put in place.

Solution: Strong interpersonal skills will be needed to convince this manager to conform to the system that has been established. His competence in Excel should be acknowledged, and the existing system reviewed to incorporate elements of his system to ensure the best options are used. Incorporating elements of this manager's system should ensure "buy in" to the company's procedure in this regard, and resolve the problem of the unnecessary reproduction of sales figures.

3 In some cases, the incorrect information is being collected from the trial balance, resulting in inaccurate sales results being submitted. An example of this is that the YTD (rather than monthly) sales results are being submitted by Sydney Branch.

Solution: Run a practical training session which demonstrates how the sales information is collated from the trial balance. This should include some sort of verification of skills at the end of the session. A section could be added to the policy and procedures manual, explaining (and perhaps illustrating with a mock trial balance) exactly which trial balance figures are used to generate the sales results collected. Two people in each branch should be trained, and sales information should always be collated by those two people. A follow-up on this area of the audit would be appropriate to check that this important problem has been rectified.

4   At Head Office level, data entry errors are occurring when information received from branches is loaded into the sales results spreadsheet.

Solution: The risk of data entry errors should be reduced by implementing a system where data is duplicated as few times as possible. In this case, why are the branches submitting handwritten figures? Sales figures could be entered into a spreadsheet at branch level, then forwarded to head office in this format, where all branch spreadsheets can be automatically combined into one. This would not only remove the opportunity for data entry errors, but would also save the time taken at head office level to input data.

5   Collated information is not getting to branch managers quickly enough from Head Office. Managers need an immediate focus on sales results in order to motivate their staff and achieve their budgets. Finding out what other branches achieved half way through the following month is almost useless.

Solution: The solution to issue 4 should also resolve the problem of timeliness, as preparation of collated sales figures will be considerably faster. Additionally, all branch managers could be forwarded the collated spreadsheet by email as soon as it is completed. Alternatively, the sales spreadsheet could be posted on the Intranet as soon as it has been updated, and all branch managers advised of this by email.

6   Some branches are not meeting organisational requirements in terms of confidentiality, with sales results being posted in clear view of all clients. When questioned about this, the managers involved did not realise this was an issue of concern, and were happy to remove the material and post it more appropriately in the staff room where it could be viewed only by staff.

Solution: A section should be added (or clarified if it already exists) to the policy and procedures manual covering the handling of this type of information. The new section should initially be circulated to all branch managers to bring their attention to it.

Index

Filing systems, 69, 147
    Active files, 69
    Card indexes, 148
    Classification systems, 150
    Inactive files, 69
    Large documentation, 148
    Non-active files, 69
    Preparing documents, 155
    Procedures, 148
    Rotary files, 148
    Semi-active files, 69
    Sorting documentation, 156
    Vertical files, 147
Folders, 137
Forms
    Leader tabs, 31
    Online, 33
    Paper-based, 30

G

General offices, 2
Graphics and presentation software, 89

H

Home based offices, 3

I

Information
    Arranging, 59
    Books and manuals, 133
    Collating spreadsheet data, 175
    Collection, 4
    Communicate effectively, 99
    Communicating, 119
    Difficulties in accessing, 131
    Disposal, 69
    Feedback, 160
    File sharing, 156
    Future needs, 176
    Help Desks, 133
    Incoming, 2
    Internet, 133
    Modification, 171, 172
    Notice boards, 134
    Organisational requirements, 53
    Organising, 86, 131
    Overload, 3
    Personal collection, 10
    Procedures, 2
    Reports, 119
    Review processes, 132
    Reviewing needs, 160
    Security, 53, 67, 68
    Seeking assistance, 132
    Selecting, 59
    Sensitive information, 129
    Sources, 51
        Agencies, 52
        Books, 51
        Courses, 52
        Internet, 51
        Libraries, 52
        Magazines and journals, 52
        Newspapers, 51
        People, 51
        Radio, 51
        TV, 51

Sources within the office, 68
Standard formats, 55
Standardised documentation, 54
Storing electronically, 136
Storing paper based information, 147
Training courses, 133
Using Microsoft Word to organise, 60
Verbal, 2
Written collection, 30
Internal mail, 34
    Circulation slips, 35
    Inter-office mail, 34
Internet, 2, 51, 79, 133, *See* also Email
    Internet Service Provider, 79
    Search engines, 51
Inter-office mail, 34
Intranet, 74, 80
IP address, 82

J

Journals, 52

L

LAN, 74
Laptops, 85
Libraries, 52
Listening skills, 14, 15
    Active listening, 16
    Encouraging, 17
    Ineffective listening, 19
    Rephrasing, 17
    Summarising, 18

M

Magazines, 52
Mail, 2
    Security, 67
Meetings, 25
    Managing meetings, 25
    Sharing information, 26
    Speaking rights, 26
    Teamwork, 26
Microsoft Outlook. *See* Outlook
Microsoft PowerPoint. *See* PowerPoint
Microsoft Word. *See* Word
Mobile phones, 77
Modems, 78
Multimedia projectors, 84
Multimedia software, 90

N

Networks, 73, 74
    Extranet, 81
    Internet, 79
    Intranet, 80
Newspapers, 51

O

Office procedures
    General offices, 2
    Home based offices, 3
    Information, 2
    Retail outlets, 2
    Salespeople, 3

Schools, 2
Office resources
  Security, 68
Office staff, 125
Outlook
  Ask a Question, 37
  Attaching files, 48
  Calendar, 36
  Contacts, 36
    Creating contacts, 46
  Control Menu Box, 37
  Creating a new message, 40
  Deleted Items, 36
  Deleting messages, 45
  Distribution lists, 46
  Email Icons, 43
  Flagging messages, 49
  Folder list, 38
  Forwarding messages, 45
  Inbox, 36, 38
  Information viewer, 37
  Managing messages, 145
  Maximize button, 37
  Menu bar, 37
  Minimize button, 37
  Notes, 36
  Organising messages, 145
  Outlook Bar, 36, 38
  Outlook Today, 36
  Outlook Window, 37
  Preview Pane, 38
  Printing messages, 44
  Reading messages, 43
  Replying to all recipients, 44
  Replying to messages, 44
  Restore, 37
  Saving attachments, 48
  Saving draft messages, 43
  Selecting messages, 45
  Sending blind copies of messages, 43
  Sending copies of messages, 42
  Sending messages, 42
  Sending messages to several people, 42
  Set a priority, 41
  Spell check, 41
  Standard toolbar, 37
  Tasks, 36
  Title bar, 37
  Viewing folders, 146

P

Pagers, 77
Peer-to-peer network, 73
People as information sources, 51
Personal collection of information, 10
  Body language, 10
  Conversation, 28
  Listening skills, 14
  Meetings, 25
  Questioning, 21
  Verbal communication, 20
Personal digital assistants, 85
Photocopiers, 83
PowerPoint
  Copying and pasting a chart, 114
  Creating a new presentation, 112
  Design templates, 114
  Logos, 112
  Navigation, 117

Presentation elements, 104
Presentation evaluation form, 169
Presenting information, 104
Starting, 110
Transitions, 114
Viewing a presentation, 110
Presentations. *See* also PowerPoint
  Action plan, 103
  Charts, 106
  Check list, 118
  Colour, 105
  Content, 104
  Delivering, 116
  Drafting, 107
  Evaluating, 118
  Logos, 106
  Objects, 106
  Pictures, 106
  Planning, 101, 102
  Text, 104
  Worksheet, 107, 108
Printers, 83

Q

Questioning techniques, 21
  Closed questions, 21
  Double questions, 23
  Leading questions, 23
  Open questions, 22

R

Radio, 51
Recycle Bin, 144
Reference books, 51
Reports, 119
  Layout, 119
Retail outlets, 2

S

Salespeople, 3
Schools, 2
Security
  Computers, 68, 69
  Disposal of information, 68, 69
  Email, 67
  Fax machines, 68
  Faxes, 67
  Information, 67
  Mail, 67
  Office resources, 68
  Photocopiers, 68
  Staff, 70
  Staff security provisions, 70
  Storage of information, 68
  Telephone, 67
Software, 72
  Accounting software, 89
  Architects, 72
  Communications, 89
  Computer aided design, 90
  Database, 88
  Dentist, 72
  Desktop publishing, 88
  Email, 89
  Government, 72
  Graphics and presentation, 89
  Medical, 72

Multimedia, 90
Spreadsheet, 87
Web browser, 82, 89
Windows, 86
Word processing, 87
Sorting documentation, 156
Spreadsheet development, 4
  Brief, 4
  Creation, 5
  Documentation, 5
  Evaluation, 5
  Evaluation form, 167, 168
  Problem, 4
  Working plan, 5, 7, 92
Spreadsheet software, 87
Spreadsheets
  Collating data, 175
  Creating, 91
  Documentation, 96
  Modification, 172
  Protection, 174
Staff
  Security, 70
Stand-alone computer systems, 73
Storage of information
  Security, 68
Styles, 60
  Applying styles, 61

T

Table of Contents, 65
  Creation, 66
Teamwork, 26
Technology, 72
Telephone
  Answering, 131
  Security, 67
Telephone networks, 78
Telephone systems, 74
  Answer phones, 74
  Mobile/Cellular phones, 77
TV, 51
Types of networks, 74

V

Verbal communication, 20
  Questioning techniques, 21

Voice, 20
Words and etiquette, 20

W

WAN, 74
Windows, 86
Windows Explorer, 136
  Address Bar, 137
  Close, 137
  Copying files, 142
  Creating new folders, 141
  Deleting files or folders, 143
  Directory tree structure, 137, 138
  Exiting, 144
  File extensions, 139
  Files, 139
  Folder, 137
  Minimize and Maximize, 137
  Moving files, 143
  Program Control Menu, 137
  Pull Down Menu Bar, 137
  Renaming files or folders, 143
  Right mouse button, 144
  Selecting files, 142
  Standard Buttons, 137
  Status bar, 137
  Title bar, 137
  Toolbars, 137
  Viewing files and folders, 140
Word
  Organising information, 60
  Outlines, 60, 62, 64, 65
  Styles, 60
  Tables of Contents, 65
Word processing software, 87
Written information
  Circulation slips, 35
  Collection, 30
  Email, 35
  Example formats, 56
  Faxes, 35
  Internal mail, 34
  Inter-office mail, 34
  Memos, 34
  Standard formats, 55
  Standardised documentation, 54
  Styles, 55
  Templates, 55